I0485604

Collective Bargaining Agreement:
The Florida State University Board of Trustees
and the
United Faculty of Florida General Faculty Bargaining Unit
2013 – 2016

Amended 2015

By

Irene Padavic, Scott Hannahs, Michael Buchler, Jack Fiorito, Robin Goodman, Nancy Kellett, Jennifer Proffitt, Tom Wazlavek, Renisha Gibbs, Michael Mattimore, Lynn Hogan, Janet Kistner, Rebecca Peterson, Amber Pursley, Lisa Scoles

ISBN: **978-1516951093**

Printed: August, 2015

TABLE OF CONTENTS

August 2015

PREAMBLE

The intent of the parties hereto in carrying out their responsibilities to negotiate the terms and conditions of employment of members of the bargaining unit is to promote the quality and effectiveness of education at the Florida State University and to maintain high standards of academic excellence in all phases of instruction, research, and service.

The Florida State University Board of Trustees, its appointed administrators, and the United Faculty of Florida strive to maintain a courteous, professional, and collegial relationship. Although differences sometimes arise, we are all committed to respectfully resolving our differences for the sake of our greater common interests and the interests of The Florida State University and the citizens of Florida. We affirm our respect for faculty rights as provided by the UFF-FSU Collective Bargaining Agreement, Florida Statutes, and the Florida Constitution, including the right to self-organization, to form, join, or assist labor unions or labor organizations or to refrain from such activity, to bargain collectively through representatives of their own choosing, and to engage in concerted activities, for the purpose of collective bargaining or other mutual aid or protection.

Article 1
RECOGNITION

1.1 Bargaining Unit.

(a) The Board recognizes the United Faculty of Florida (UFF) as the exclusive representative for the bargaining unit certified by the Public Employees Relations Commission in Case Number EL-2003-038 (October 24, 2003) and reflected in Certification Order Number 1438 as clarified in Case Number UC-2013-002 (April 2, 2013). This bargaining unit is the Faculty Bargaining Unit.

(b) The Board recognizes the UFF as the exclusive representative, solely for the purpose of collective bargaining with respect to wages, hours, and other terms and conditions of employment as specifically set forth in this Agreement, for all individuals in the bargaining unit described in the certification as amended.

(c) Attached as Appendix "A" is the listing of position classifications included in the Faculty Bargaining Unit.

1.2 Bargaining Unit Position Classifications.

(a) Creation of a New Classification.

(1) The Board may create new position classifications with job \duties including the creation, dissemination, or presentation of knowledge only after negotiations with the UFF to determine the nature and necessity of the new position classification and whether it will be designated within or outside the bargaining unit.

Article 1
RECOGNITION

(2) All new position classifications with job duties including a substantial teaching or research component shall be designated within the bargaining unit.

(b) Disputes Over General Classifications.

(1) If the Board wishes to revise the specifications of an existing class so that its bargaining unit designation may need to be changed, it shall notify the UFF regarding such new designation

(2) Within thirty (30) days following such notification, the UFF may request a meeting with the Board for the purpose of discussing the designation. If, following such discussion, an agreement cannot be reached, the Board and the UFF shall request that the Florida Public Employees Relations Commission resolve the dispute through unit clarification proceedings.

(c) Disputes Over Classifications of Individuals.

(1) A faculty member or the UFF may request a review of the appropriateness of a faculty member's classification by the appropriate University office.

(2) In case of disagreement with the results of the review, the parties shall proceed to a discussion of the matter in accordance with Article 2, Consultation.

(3) If the UFF believes the classification represents an error that may potentially affect the broader composition of the bargaining unit, the UFF may request that the Florida Public Employees Relations Commission resolve the dispute through unit clarification proceedings.

(d) Reclassification of Faculty Members to a Non-Unit Classification.

(1) Except in cases in which a faculty member voluntarily accepts a position already outside the Faculty Bargaining Unit, faculty members shall be provided written notice ninety (90) days in advance, where practicable, with a copy to the local UFF Chapter, when the Board proposes to reclassify the faculty member to a classification which is not contained in the Faculty Bargaining Unit.

(2) The faculty member may request a review of such action consistent with the provisions of Section 1.2.

(3) The UFF may discuss such action pursuant to Article 2, Consultation.

(4) If the UFF believes the classification represents an error that may potentially affect the broader composition of the bargaining unit, the UFF may request that the Florida Public Employees Relations Commission resolve the dispute through unit clarification proceedings.

(5) No faculty member shall be reclassified to a classification that is not contained in the Faculty Bargaining Unit for the purpose of denying the faculty member rights or protections under this Agreement. A faculty member may pursue a timely grievance over any contract violation alleged to have occurred prior to the reclassification becoming effective. A grievance filed under this section will entitle the grievant to the remedies otherwise available to a unit employee under this contract.

1.3 Board Rules and Policies.

(a) No existing, new or amended Board rule, policy, or resolution shall apply to faculty members if it conflicts with a provision of this Agreement.

(b) The Board shall provide to the local UFF Chapter an advance copy of any proposed rule or policy.

(1) The Board shall provide the advance copy of a proposed rule as soon as practicable but no later than the required date of publication of the initial public notice of a proposed rule under the provisions of the Administrative Procedure Act. With respect to a rule adopted pursuant to the emergency provisions of the Administrative Procedure Act, an advance copy shall be provided as far in advance of its effective date as is feasible under the circumstances.

(2) The advance copy of a policy shall be provided to the UFF local Chapter as soon as practicable prior to its effective date so as to permit the UFF to seek consultation with respect to it. If the UFF requests consultation with the Board or representatives about a proposed policy impacting faculty terms and conditions of employment within thirty (30) days of receipt of the advance copy, then the policy shall not take effect until after the consultation. If the UFF has not requested a consultation on the proposed policy within thirty (30) days of receipt of the advance copy, the Board may proceed to implement the policy.

(c) If the Board or a committee or subcommittee of the Board has scheduled public hearings on any Board action that would conflict with an express term of this Agreement, the UFF shall be explicitly notified and provided the opportunity to address the matter.

(d) If any proposed rule, policy, or resolution would modify an express term of this Agreement, the Board or its designee shall engage in collective bargaining with respect to the change upon the UFF's request. Policies bearing on a matter that is a proper subject of collective bargaining shall be made only through negotiation and agreement with the UFF.

1.4 Board of Trustees Meetings—Agenda and Minutes.

(a) The Board shall furnish to the UFF a copy of the agenda of each Board meeting or Board committee or subcommittee meeting at the time those agendas are made available to members of the Board or a committee of the Board.

(b) The Board shall complete collective bargaining negotiations with the UFF prior to taking action on an agenda item that would alter a term or condition of bargaining unit employment and is a mandatory subject of bargaining.

(c) The Board shall furnish to the UFF a copy of the public minutes of Board or committee meetings at the time they are made available to the members of the Board or committee.

1.5 Right to Hear Views.

(a) The Board may meet with any individual or organization to hear views on any matter, provided, however, that policies bearing on any such matter which is a proper subject of collective bargaining shall be made only through negotiation and agreement with the UFF.

Article 2
CONSULTATION

(b) If the Board meets with a group or organization to hear views or to discuss a matter that is a proper subject of collective bargaining, a UFF representative shall be permitted to address the subject.

(c) Faculty Orientations. At all orientation meetings expressly for faculty members the UFF shall be permitted to make presentations of reasonable length and to distribute informational material from the UFF.

Article 2
CONSULTATION

2.1 Consultations.

(a) Up to six (6) representatives from the University shall meet with up to six (6) UFF Representatives to discuss matters pertinent to the implementation or administration of this Agreement, University administration actions affecting terms and conditions of employment, or any other mutually agreeable matters.

(b) Such meetings shall occur at least twice (2) per semester during the academic year and once (1) during the summer unless the University President and the UFF agree otherwise. At least two (2) consultation meetings per year will take place with the University President. The Provost or the Vice President for Faculty Development and Advancement will attend meetings when the President is absent. Additional consultations may be scheduled by mutual agreement.

(c) The University President and the UFF shall submit a written list of agenda items no less than one (1) week in advance of the meeting.

(d) The Board and the UFF understand and agree that such meetings may be used to resolve problems regarding the implementation and administration of the Agreement. However, such meetings shall not constitute or be used for the purpose of collective bargaining, unless the Board and the UFF agree otherwise. An accurate record of the proceedings of such meetings shall be maintained.

2.2 Contract Administration Meetings. The BOT and UFF shall schedule contract administration meetings as needed and as mutually agreed upon.

Article 3
UFF RIGHTS

3.1 Use of Facilities and Services.

(a) The UFF shall have the right to use university facilities for meetings and all other services on terms no less favorable than other organizations such as student organizations, honor societies, fraternities, sororities and alumni associations.

(b) The Board shall provide the UFF with the same office as the University is currently providing, unless the Board and the UFF mutually agree to other arrangements.

(c) The UFF's current use of university facilities and other services shall not be diminished.

3.2 Communications.

(a) UFF may post bulletins and notices relevant to its position as the collective bargaining agent on a reasonable number of existing bulletin boards.

(1) Specific locations shall be mutually selected by the Board or its representatives and the local UFF Chapter in the course of consultation pursuant to Article 2, Consultation.

(2) All materials placed on the designated bulletin boards shall bear the date of posting, the signature of the UFF official authorizing the posting and may be removed by the Board or its representatives after having been posted for a period of thirty (30) days. In addition, such bulletin boards may not be used for election campaigns for public office.

(b) The Board shall place a link to the web site of the local UFF in mutually agreed upon places on the university web site.

(c) UFF faculty and faculty representatives may use existing university e-mail listservs to communicate electronically with faculty and the Board. In the event the UFF seeks to establish a new listserv it shall be a subject of consultation pursuant to Article 2, Consultation. Faculty who are e-mail recipients of the listserv shall have the right to have themselves removed from the listserv upon their written request.

(d) UFF may use the campus mails, subject to all applicable regulations of the United States Postal Service. The UFF may also use e-mail and any electronic message system, at no cost. The mails may not be used for election campaigns for public office, except that the UFF may announce endorsements made by the UFF or its affiliates.

(e) The Board shall not make reprisals of any kind against faculty members for engaging in any of the forms of communication described in this section.

3.3 Leave of Absence -- Union Activity.

(a) At the written request of the UFF, provided no later than May 1 of the year prior to the beginning of the academic year when such leave is to become effective, a full-time or part-time leave of absence for the academic year shall be granted to up to three (3) faculty members designated by the UFF for the purpose of carrying out UFF's obligations in representing faculty members and administering this Agreement, including lobbying and other political representation. Such leave shall also be granted to up to three (3) faculty members for the entire summer term, upon written request by the UFF provided no later than March 15. The Board may refuse to honor any of the leave of absence requests if they are submitted after the deadline.

(b) No more than one faculty member per fifteen (15) faculty members per department/unit need be granted such leave at any one time, unless the Board and the UFF agree otherwise.

(c) The UFF shall reimburse the Board for the faculty member's salary, fringe benefits, and retirement.

(d) Faculty members on full-time leave under this paragraph shall be eligible to receive salary increases. Faculty members on less than full-time leave under this paragraph shall be eligible to receive salary increases on the same basis as other faculty members.

(e) The Board shall not be liable for the acts or omissions of said faculty members during the leave and the UFF shall hold the Board harmless for any such acts or omissions, including the cost of defending against such claims.

(f) An employee on such leave shall not be evaluated for this activity. However, such activity shall be considered university service, and the Board shall not use such activity against the faculty member in making personnel decisions.

3.4 Release Time.
(a) The Board agrees to provide a total of sixteen (16) units of release time during each twelve-month period beginning with the fall semester of each year. It will provide the release time to full-time faculty members designated by the UFF for the purpose of carrying out the UFF's obligations in representing faculty members and administering this Agreement. The UFF may designate faculty members to receive release time during the academic year, subject to the following conditions:
(1) In departments/units with fifteen (15) or fewer faculty members, no more than one unit of release time shall be assigned without consent of the department/unit supervisor.
(2) The UFF shall provide the Board with a list of designees for the fall and spring terms no later than May 1 preceding the academic year. No fewer than four (4) units and no greater than six (6) units will be designated for each term. Upon approval of the designees by the Board, the designees shall serve for one (1) academic year or one term as designated by the UFF. Changes for the spring semester may be made upon written notification submitted by the UFF to the Board no later than October 15.

(b) Release Time Units.
(1) Each "unit" of release time shall consist of a 25% reduction in the academic assignment per fall or spring semester for faculty members. Prior to the UFF notifying the Vice President for Faculty Development and Advancement of the list of designees, the potential designees shall consult with the chair or other immediate supervisor and determine the distribution of the reduction among teaching, research and service assignments so as to best serve the interests of the faculty member and the University. The reduction shall normally come from the teaching assignment, for faculty with teaching responsibilities. Exceptions shall be justified in a written statement signed by the faculty member and the immediate supervisor.

Where the faculty member has a teaching assignment after the reduction in academic assignment and the schedule of classes will allow, the University shall arrange for Tuesday – Thursday teaching schedules for faculty members who are designated to receive release time for collective bargaining.

(2) A faculty member may receive more than one "unit" of release time per semester. Release time shall be used for conducting UFF business, and shall not be used for lobbying or other political representation. Leave for lobbying or other political representation may be purchased by the UFF pursuant to Section 3.3.

(c) Faculty members who are on leave of any kind, other than leave pursuant to Section 3.3, shall not be eligible to receive release time.

(d) The Board may refuse to honor any of the release time requests submitted after the deadline.

(e) Faculty members on release time shall be eligible for salary increases on the same basis as other faculty members. Their release time activities shall not be evaluated, but such release time shall be considered university service and the Board shall not use such activity against the faculty in making personnel decisions.

(f) Faculty members on release time shall retain all rights and responsibilities as other faculty members but shall not be considered representatives of the Board for any activities undertaken on behalf of the UFF. The UFF agrees to hold the Board harmless for any claims arising from such activities, including the cost of defending against such claims.

(g) Summer.
(1) The Board agrees to provide UFF at least four (4) units and no more than six (6) units of release time assignments in increments of 0.25 FTE over thirteen (13) weeks, but not more than 16 units per year in accordance with 3.4(a) above. A faculty member may be designated for more than one unit increment. No more than one faculty member per fifteen (15) faculty members per department/unit may be designated to receive such release time, unless agreed to by the department supervisor.
(2) The UFF shall provide the Board with a list of requested designees no later than April 7th of the academic year preceding the summer term.
(3) All other provisions contained in Section 3.4, except 3.4(a) and (b), shall apply to summer release time.

Article 4
BOARD RIGHTS

4.1 Policy. The Board and the UFF agree that the Board shall have the rights, powers, and authority vested in it by law, including the right to plan, manage, administer, and control Florida State University in carrying out the ordinary and customary functions of management.

Article 5
ACADEMIC FREEDOM AND RESPONSIBILITY

4.2 Limitations.

(a) All such rights, powers, and authority are subject to those limitations imposed by this Agreement.

(b) Only violations of such limitations shall be subject to Article 20, Grievance Procedure and Arbitration.

4.3 Other Rights Recognized. Nothing in this article shall limit or waive the right of the UFF or any faculty member to:

(a) Seek redress before the Public Employee Relations Commission (PERC) for violations of the Public Employees Relations Act; or

(b) Initiate federal or state court actions for violations of federal or state laws.

Article 5
ACADEMIC FREEDOM AND RESPONSIBILITY

5.1 Policy. Academic freedom and responsibility are essential to the integrity of a true university and are rooted in a conception of the University as a community of scholars united in the pursuit of truth and wisdom in an atmosphere of tolerance and freedom.

(a) The Board and the UFF shall maintain, encourage, protect, and promote full academic freedom in teaching, research/creative activities, and professional, public, and University service. The Board and the UFF also affirm that academic freedom is accompanied by corresponding faculty and Administration responsibilities, arising from the nature of the educational process.

(b) As to matters outside the area of the faculty member's scholarly interest, the faculty member has the right to enjoy the same freedoms as other individuals, including political rights and privileges, without fear of institutional censorship or discipline.

(c) In order to ensure within the University an atmosphere of academic freedom and confidence,

(1) The Board or its representatives shall not apply any provision in this Agreement in such a way as to violate a faculty member's academic freedom or constitutional rights, including constitutionally protected freedom of expression, or to penalize a faculty member for the legitimate exercise of those freedoms.

(2) The Board shall protect any member of the faculty against influences, from within or without the University, which would restrict the faculty member in the exercise of these freedoms.

5.2 Academic Freedom. A faculty member shall be free to discuss all relevant matters in the classroom, to explore all avenues of scholarship, research, and creative expression, to speak freely on all matters of University governance, and to speak, write, or act in an atmosphere of freedom and confidence, all without fear of institutional censorship, reprisal, or discipline and without regard to whether the expression is verbal, written, or electronic.

(a) Teaching and Research/Creative Activities. Faculty members shall have the freedom to:

(1) Present and discuss, frankly and forthrightly, academic subjects, including controversial material relevant to the course of instruction.

(2) Select instructional materials, define course content, and determine grades, subject to a department's ordinary control over curriculum. The grade a faculty member determines for a student's performance shall not be changed without the faculty member's consent, except in accord with specified procedures established by the Faculty Senate.

(3) Freely engage in scholarly and creative activity and publish the results.

(b) Service. Service includes, but is not limited to, participation in the governance processes of the University, which is a fundamental aspect of academic freedom. Faculty shall have freedom to present and discuss, frankly and forthrightly, academic policy, University governance, or other matters pertaining to the health of the University.

(c) The rights provided in this Article shall fully extend to all bargaining unit members, regardless of whether their primary responsibilities include teaching or research.

5.3 Academic Responsibility of the Faculty. Academic Responsibility implies the competent performance of academic duties and obligations and the commitment to support the responsible exercise of freedom by others. Members of the faculty are expected to:

(a) Observe and uphold the ethical standards of their disciplines in the pursuit and communication of scientific and scholarly knowledge.

(b) Treat students, staff and colleagues in a manner consistent with the provisions of Sections 5.1 and 5.2 and Article 6, Nondiscrimination.

(c) Respect the integrity of the evaluation process, evaluating students, staff, and colleagues fairly according to the criteria the evaluation process specifies.

(d) Represent oneself as a spokesperson for the University only when specifically authorized to do so.

(e) Participate, as appropriate, in the system of shared governance, especially at the department level.

(f) Manifest integrity in their dealings with colleagues, be willing to share responsibilities and contribute equitably to the group tasks they are assigned.

(g) Observe the published regulations of the University, provided they do not contravene academic freedom or the faculty member's right to criticize and seek revision of those regulations.

Article 5
ACADEMIC FREEDOM AND RESPONSIBILITY

5.4 Academic Responsibility of the Board. Academic Responsibility implies a commitment to foster actively within the University a climate favorable to the responsible exercise of freedom. Therefore, it is the responsibility of the Board and the University Administration to:

(a) Sustain and defend academic freedom, taking positive actions to ensure that academic freedom is not chilled or compromised by harassment, censorship, reprisals, unfair employment decisions, or prohibited discrimination as defined in Article 6, Nondiscrimination.

(b) Adhere to principles of shared governance, which require that in the development of academic policies and processes the professional judgments of faculty members are of primary importance.

(c) Respect the integrity of the evaluation process, evaluating faculty fairly and accurately according to the criteria the evaluation process specifies.

(d) Prohibit persons who are not authorized students, authorized instructional staff, or authorized officials of the University from entering or interrupting faculty classrooms or laboratories, except with prior permission from the responsible faculty member or during legitimate emergencies. To immediately address a situation, faculty members may ask students to leave when their behavior is disruptive. The FSU Police Department will respond directly at any time and can be called if a faculty member believes a disruption might pose a risk to his or her personal safety or the safety of others. University administrators are also available to the faculty member to assist in addressing disruptive behavior, and faculty are encouraged to seek their assistance.

(e) Just cause to discipline a faculty member under Article 16 for actions related to self-defense or the defense of others will be judged according to whether the response was reasonable under the totality of the facts and circumstances known to the faculty member at the time of the incident.

(f) The University shall make a reasonable effort to notify faculty members of public-records requests made known to the General Counsel's office, the Office of Human Resources, or the Office of the Vice President for Faculty Development and Advancement that seek access to the faculty member's FSU email accounts, voicemail, or written content.

(1) The University shall provide guidance to chairs and other administrators on the handling of public records requests.

(2) The University shall notify the affected faculty member within ten days of receiving the request and prior to fulfilling the request.

(3) Any retained copies of the information provided to the requester shall be made available for review by the faculty member at no cost. A faculty member may request a copy of the information provided to the requestor at cost.

(4) The University shall provide guidance to faculty regarding its records retention policy.

Article 6
NONDISCRIMINATION

6.1   Statement of Intent.

(a) The Board and the UFF recognize their obligations under federal and state laws, rules, and regulations prohibiting discrimination or harassment.

(b) The Board and the UFF affirm their support for the concepts of diversity and affirmative action. They recognize that the purpose of affirmative action is to provide equal opportunity in employment. The Board and the UFF shall implement programs, policies, and practices to facilitate the recruitment, appointment, retention and professional development of women and minorities. This statement of intent is not subject to Article 20, Grievance Procedure and Arbitration.

6.2   Policy.

(a) Discrimination.

(1) Personnel decisions shall be based solely on job-related criteria and performance.

(2) Furthermore, neither the Board nor the UFF shall discriminate against any faculty member based upon race, color, sex, religious creed, national origin, age, veteran status, disability, political affiliation, marital status, sexual orientation, gender identity or gender expression, nor shall the Board or the UFF abridge any rights of faculty members related to union activity granted under Chapter 447, Florida Statutes, including but not limited to the right to assist or to refrain from assisting the UFF, or the exercise of any rights under this Agreement.

(3) Should state or federal law establish any additional protected category for claims of discrimination during the term of this Agreement, the Board and the UFF agree to modify the Agreement pursuant to Section 30.2

(b) Harassment.

(1) Some types of workplace harassment may constitute discrimination.

(2) The faculty shall be protected from workplace harassment that is premised upon sex/gender or other protected classes of individuals.

(3) In Meritor Savings Bank v. Vinson, 477 U.S. 57 (1986), the United States Supreme Court recognized two types of sexual harassment in employment: quid-pro-quo harassment and hostile-environment harassment.

a.   The Supreme Court defined hostile-environment harassment as occurring only when "the workplace is permeated with 'discriminatory intimidation, ridicule, and insult' that is 'sufficiently severe or pervasive to alter the conditions of the victim's employment and create an abusive working environment'" (Harris v. Forklift Systems, Inc., 510 U.S. 17, (1993), quoting Meritor, 477 U.S. AT 65, 67).

b.   The EEOC Guidelines provide that "'quid pro quo harassment' occurs when 'submission to or rejection of [unwelcome sexual] conduct by an individual is used as the basis for employment decisions affecting such individual'" (EEOC, "Policy Guidance on Current

Issues of Sexual Harassment," No. N-915-050 [March 19, 1990], quoting 29 CFR 1604.11A[2-3]).

       c. Title VII does not proscribe all conduct of a sexual nature in the workplace (EEOC, "Policy Guidance on Current Issues of Sexual Harassment," No.N-915-050, 3/19/90). However, even consensual sexual relationships may involve a conflict of interest. Such conflicts of interest are subject to the provisions of Article 19.

       (4) In addition to the Board and the UFF's concern with respect to sexual harassment between employees, the Board and the UFF recognize the potential for this form of illegal discrimination involving students, including unwelcome sexual advances, requests for sexual favors, or other verbal or physical conduct of a sexual nature that constitutes sexual harassment.

       (5) Furthermore, the Board and the UFF recognize that sexual relationships between faculty and students, even if consensual, may become exploitative and especially so when a student's academic work, residential life, or athletic endeavors are supervised or evaluated by the faculty member.

       (6) Policies and regulations regarding harassment are intended to protect individuals from discrimination, not to regulate the content of speech, or restrict the academic freedom or free speech rights of faculty.

6.3   Investigation of Complaints of Discrimination or Harassment. Charges of discrimination, including complaints of harassment, shall be promptly investigated according to the following:

    (a) No retaliation shall be made by a faculty member, the Board or the UFF against any party, witness or representative arising from their good faith participation in the investigation process.

    (b) The Board shall take appropriate remedial measures to correct any finding of discrimination or harassment that is found.

    (c) The remedial measures shall not adversely affect the faculty member who was found to be the object of discrimination or harassment.

    (d) In the process of investigating discrimination or harassment the conduct shall be considered in the context of the entire circumstances.

    (e) The investigative report shall contain at least the following information:
       (1) The nature of the complaint;
       (2) All formal statements by the parties;
       (3) A summary of the findings; and
       (4) A conclusion as to whether there is cause to determine that discrimination or harassment has occurred.

    (f) In instances where no finding of discrimination or harassment is made, no record of the complaint shall be placed in the faculty member's evaluation file unless the faculty member requests in writing that a record of the complete investigation be placed in the evaluation file.

(g) No faculty member shall be disciplined for discrimination or harassment until the investigation is complete and a finding of discrimination or harassment has been issued. The Board may determine that non-disciplinary action is appropriate pending the completion of the investigation. The faculty member may be placed on administrative leave pursuant to Article 17 of this Agreement during the investigation.

(h) Disciplinary actions shall follow the policy of progressive discipline, pursuant to Article 16, Disciplinary Action.

6.4   Access to Documents. No faculty member shall be refused a request to inspect and copy documents relating to any claim of discrimination to which the faculty member is a party, except for records that are exempt from the provisions of the Public Records Act, Chapter 119, Florida Statutes.

6.5   Grievance Procedures.
    (a) Claims of discrimination or harassment brought against the Board may be presented as grievances pursuant to Article 20, Grievance Procedure and Arbitration. However, no grievance may be maintained under this section if the faculty member has also initiated a complaint arising from the same issue(s) filed with any court or fair employment practices agency, except as specifically provided for in Article 20. This article cannot be relied upon to grieve issues that are not a violation of a provision of this Agreement.

    (b) Appeals of adverse employment decisions made against faculty accused of discrimination or harassment may be presented as grievances pursuant to Article 20, Grievance Procedure and Arbitration.

Article 7
ACCESS TO DOCUMENTS

7.1   Board and University Documents.
    (a) Upon request, within three (3) business days or as soon thereafter as possible, the Board shall provide the UFF with a print or electronic copy of documents necessary to administer grievances and other provisions of this Agreement or otherwise carry out the UFF's obligations as the certified bargaining agent for the faculty. Alternatively, upon mutual agreement, the Board may provide the UFF with the specific URL addresses where the materials requested can be found.

    (b) No later than when they are made available to the participants, the Board shall provide the UFF with an electronic copy of the agenda and minutes of meetings that may bear on the terms and conditions of employment of faculty members, including meetings (and subcommittee meetings) of the Board, the Council of Presidents, and the Council of Deans.

(c) The Board shall ensure that a copy of the following documents is made available in an easily accessible location in Strozier Library or by links on the University web site:

(1) The minutes of the meetings of the Council of Presidents;

(2) The minutes of the meetings of the Board and its committees;

(3) Board rules published under the Administrative Procedure Act;

(4) The University's operating budget and the previous year's Expenditure Analysis;

(5) The FSU BOT–UFF Agreement and all supplements to the Agreement; and

(6) Any other University policies and procedures affecting faculty terms or conditions of employment.

(d) All copies of materials, and access to materials, shall be provided without cost.

7.2   Salary Records Access. Upon request, within three (3) business days or as soon thereafter as possible the Board shall provide the UFF with an electronic copy of faculty employment records reflecting the annual salary increases provided to faculty and any other necessary information for bargaining and for verifying compliance with the terms of the salary article (Article 23) of this Agreement.

7.3   Bargaining Unit Member List. Within seven (7) days of the beginning of each semester, the Board shall provide the UFF with an electronic list including name, department/unit, position code, title/rank, e-mail address, contact telephone number, and contact mailing address for each faculty member in the bargaining unit.

Article 8
APPOINTMENT

8.1   Policy. The Board, working with the faculty of each department/unit shall determine standards, qualifications, and criteria so as to fill appointment vacancies in the bargaining unit with the best possible candidates. In furtherance of this aim:

(a) The Board shall, through the appropriate departments/units, advertise such appointment vacancies.

(b) Committees composed of members of the faculty of the department/unit shall receive applications and screen candidates.

(c) The Board, working together with the faculty of the department/unit, shall make such appointments as appropriate under the established standards, qualifications, and criteria, consistent with their commitment to implement programs, policies, and practices to facilitate the recruitment, appointment, and retention of a diverse faculty.

8.2   Vacancies.

(a) Bargaining unit vacancies shall be advertised through appropriate professional channels unless a waiver of announcement has been approved by the President or representative in the event of exceptions caused by unanticipated and compelling circumstances (see "Waiver of Posting" in The Guide for Hiring Officials and Search and Screening Committees, 2005 edition). Faculty members of lower or equivalent ranks, relations of faculty members, retired faculty members, and faculty members who are local residents shall not be disqualified from consideration or otherwise disadvantaged in the hiring process.

(b) Prior to any discussion or negotiation of the candidate's initial salary, the candidate for a new or vacant position shall be informed of the salaries of faculty members in the department/unit, or of salaries of faculty members employed by the University in the same job classification, as appropriate.

(c) In all decisions to hire a candidate to fill a bargaining unit vacancy, the appropriate administrator(s) shall, whenever possible, act in accordance with the recommendations that have resulted from the review of candidates by faculty members in the affected departments/units.

8.3   Commitment to developing and maintaining a tenured faculty. The Board agrees that it is in the best interests of the University, the faculty, and the students to maximize the ratio of tenured and tenure-accruing E&G appointments to the number of specialized (non-tenure-accruing) E&G appointments, among those appointments including significant teaching responsibilities.
(a) Two weeks after the first day of class in the Fall semester, the Board shall notify the UFF of the number of credit hours taught in the University during the previous academic year, broken down by the position class code of the instructor. It shall also report the current number of tenured and tenure-earning faculty (TTF) FTEs and the current number of specialized faculty (SF) FTEs in the General Faculty bargaining unit, broken down by source of funding (i.e., E&G, C&G).

(b) Non-tenure accruing faculty position classifications shall only be used for faculty members whose duty assignments are specialized, so as to be predominantly teaching, predominantly research, or predominantly service in support of teaching or research, as specified in Article 9. Other faculty members, whose duty assignments combine a significant amount of both teaching and other scholarly activities shall be appointed in tenured or tenure-accruing classifications.

8.4   Employment Contract. All appointments shall be made on a University employment contract and signed by the Board or representative and the faculty member. The employment contract may include informational addenda reflecting special terms and conditions agreed to between the parties, except that such addenda may not abridge the faculty member's rights or benefits provided in this Agreement. All appointments for faculty members appointed for the entire academic year shall begin on the same date. The University employment contract shall contain the following elements:

Article 8
APPOINTMENT

(a) Date(s) executed;

(b) Professional Classification System title, class code, rank, and appointment status;

(c) Department, program, college, or other employment unit;

(d) The starting and ending dates of the appointment;

(e) A statement that the position is (1) tenured, (2) tenure-earning (specifying prior service in another institution to be credited toward tenure), (3) fixed-term multi-year appointment (MYA, as defined in article 8.6), or (4) other non-tenure-earning.

(f) The following statement, if the appointment is not subject to the notice provisions of Article 12: "Your employment under this contract will cease on the date indicated. No further notice of cessation of employment is required.";

(g) Percent of full-time employment ("FTE") assigned;

(h) Salary rate;

(i) Principal place of employment;

(j) Special conditions of employment;

(k) A statement that the appointment is subject to the Constitution and laws of the State of Florida and the United States, the rules of the Board and this Agreement;

(l) The statement: "The BOT-UFF Collective Bargaining Agreement (Article 6) provides that personnel decisions shall be based solely on job-related criteria and performance, and prohibits discrimination or harassment against any faculty member. Claims against the Board, charging such discrimination, may be presented as grievances pursuant to Article 20, Grievance Procedure and Arbitration";

(m) A statement informing the faculty member of the obligation to report outside activity and conflict of interest under the provisions of Article 19 of the Collective Bargaining Agreement;

(n) A statement that the faculty member's signature on the standard employment contract shall not be deemed a waiver of the right to process a grievance with respect thereto in compliance with Article 20, Grievance Procedure and Arbitration;

(o) The statement: "A copy of the BOT-UFF Collective Bargaining Agreement will be provided to you."

(p) The following statement, if the appointment has been approved by the faculty of an academic department/unit with a degree program for use of the honorific title appropriate to the classification containing the word "professor," or in the case of Panama City Campus faculty, meets alternative criteria as outlined by the criteria and procedures specified in Appendix J of this Agreement: "Honorific Title: (Assistant/Associate/Full) (Teaching/Research) Professor as approved by the faculty of (the department)." For example "Associate Teaching Professor".

8.5   Appointments.
  (a) Change in Appointments.
      (1) A faculty member serving on a calendar year appointment may request an academic year appointment, or an annual leave-accruing appointment of less than twelve (12) months but more than nine (9) months. Similarly, a faculty member serving on an academic-year appointment may request a calendar-year appointment or an annual-leave-accruing appointment of less than twelve (12) months but more than nine (9) months. The President or representative shall carefully consider such requests, although staffing considerations and other relevant University needs may prevent a request being granted.

      (2) Upon approval by the President or representative, and assuming that the assigned responsibilities remain substantially the same, a faculty member's base salary shall be adjusted by 81.8 percent when changing from a calendar-year to an academic- year appointment or by 122.2 percent when changing from an academic-year to a calendar-year appointment. For a faculty member whose appointment was previously changed from an academic-year to calendar-year appointment at a salary adjustment other than 122.2 percent or from a calendar-year to academic-year appointment at a salary adjustment other than 81.8 percent, the percent which is the reciprocal of the percent previously used shall be used to make the salary adjustment.

      (3) Upon approval of a change from a calendar-year appointment to an annual-leave-accruing appointment of less than twelve (12) months but more than nine (9) months, the faculty member's salary shall be adjusted to a percent of the calendar-year base salary that is mathematically proportionate.

      (4) Under special circumstances the FTE or the duration of the appointment may be altered at the request of the faculty member by written agreement between the appropriate administrator and the faculty member.
            a.   The reduction in FTE shall reflect a tangible reduction in assigned duties for one or more elements of the faculty member's assignment (e.g., teaching, research, and service) as specified in Article 9.
            b.   The written agreement between the faculty member and the appropriate administrator will contain the duration of time for which the alteration will take place.
            c.   If a faculty member in a tenure-earning appointment receives a reduction in FTE or term of appointment, the time credited toward tenure for the term of the reduced appointment shall be adjusted appropriately.

  (b) Summer Appointments.
      (1) Policy.

Article 8
APPOINTMENT

a. The normal nine (9)-month (academic year) faculty contract shall be for thirty-nine (39) consecutive weeks and a supplemental summer contract may be offered for all or part of the remaining year.

b. The faculty of each department/unit shall develop written criteria and a rotation policy for offering supplemental summer appointments in a fair and equitable manner. The criteria and rotation policy shall be posted in each department/unit.

c. The decision about which courses to offer will be based on programmatic needs, student demand, and budget availability.

d. Supplemental summer appointments shall be offered equitably and as appropriate to qualified faculty members, not later than five weeks prior to the beginning of the appointment in accordance with written criteria. If additional summer appointments become available, qualified faculty members will be offered these appointments in accordance with written criteria.

e. Faculty members must specify whether they want to teach during the summer within two weeks of their chair's request for faculty teaching preferences.

f. A faculty member who obtains his or her own summer employment (e.g., a research grant or other award) shall not be omitted from the consideration for subsequent supplemental appointments because of such employment.

g. Supplemental summer assignments shall be offered to qualified faculty members before anyone who is not a faculty member.

(2) Compensation. A faculty member shall receive approximately the same total compensation for teaching a course during a supplemental summer appointment as the faculty member received for teaching the same course, or a course similar in credit hours, size, and content, during the academic year, regardless of the length of the supplemental summer appointment. For example, if a 9 month faculty member was paid at 25% for teaching a three-hour course in the Fall or Spring term, then the faculty member shall receive 12.5% of the faculty member's base salary for teaching one 3-hour course, 16.7% for teaching one 4-hour course, and pay for other courses shall be prorated accordingly.

(c) Dual Compensation Appointments. Dual compensation is defined as compensation from the University for any duties (including work activities previously designated as overload) in excess of a full appointment (1.0 FTE). Dual compensation appointments within the University shall be offered equitably and as appropriate to qualified faculty members in sufficient time to allow voluntary acceptance or rejection.

(1) Duties and responsibilities assigned by the University to a faculty member that are in addition to the available established FTE for the position shall be compensated through OPS, not Salary.

(2) Duties and responsibilities assigned by the University to a faculty member that do not exceed the available established FTE for the position shall be compensated through the payment of Salary, not OPS.

(3) No faculty member shall be required to accept a dual compensation appointment. Dual compensation appointments shall be offered to qualified faculty members before anyone who is not a faculty member.

(d) Visiting Appointments. A "visiting" appointment is one made to a person having appropriate professional qualifications but not expected to be available for more than a limited period, or to a person in a position which the University Administration does not expect to be available for more than a limited period, or to a person who was selected for a regular appointment according to the process specified in Section 8.2 but could not immediately be appointed to the position for which she or he was selected. A visiting appointment may be offered in single year contracts not to exceed a total of three (3) consecutive years, except in rare cases. No faculty member with a visiting appointment shall be given a regular appointment without having been selected for the position according to the process specified in Section 8.2.

(e) Adjunct Appointments. Adjuncts shall be employed only when faculty are not available for assignment. Such appointment is for one academic term at a time and is ordinarily paid on a per course basis or, in cases of non-instructional appointments, on a per activity basis. Adjunct appointments may not be for more than 50% of the time throughout an academic year or full-time for more than twenty-six weeks of an academic year. The use of adjuncts shall, upon the request of the UFF Chapter representatives, be a subject of consultation under the provisions of Article 2.

8.6   Fixed-term Multi-Year Appointments. A fixed-term multi-year appointment (MYA) is an appointment of contingent duration, consisting of an initial multi-year fixed-term that is extendible as described below in Section 8.6(a).

(a) Fixed-term multi-year appointments shall only be offered to faculty members in the following position classifications:

(1) For the ranks of University Librarian, Teaching Faculty III, Instructional Specialist III, Senior Research Associate, Curator, and Research Faculty III, an MYA shall be offered with a term of four (4) years. Such a faculty member shall be reviewed during the second year of her/his contract and either reappointed with a four-year MYA or issued a notice of non-reappointment. Notices of reappointment or non-reappointment shall be issued by the end of the second year of the contract.

(2) For the ranks of Associate University Librarian, Teaching Faculty II, Instructional Specialist II, Associate in Research, Associate Curator, and Research Faculty II, an MYA shall be offered with a term of two (2) years. Such a faculty member shall be reviewed during the first year of her/his contract and either reappointed with a two-year MYA, or issued, a notice of non-reappointment. Notices of reappointment and non-reappointment shall be issued by the end of the first year of the contract.

(b) Annual Evaluation. Each faculty member on a continuing multi-year appointment will be evaluated annually pursuant to Article 10.

(c) Contract Extension. Unless an MYA faculty member receives a timely notice of non-reappointment as described in Sec. 8.6(a), the faculty member will receive a new MYA as described in Sec. 8.6(a). If the faculty member has an administrative code, the extension does not necessarily extend to continuation of the administrative code. In cases of voluntary resignation, retirement, removal for just cause (as in 16.1), layoff, or non-reappointment, no contract extension will be given.

(d) Probation. If a MYA faculty member receives a "Does Not Meet FSU's High Expectations" rating on the Annual Evaluation Summary Form, he or she will be placed on one-year probation. No contract extension will be added to his or her appointment for the duration of the probationary period. A Performance Improvement Plan (PIP) shall be required.

(1) The Performance Improvement Plan shall be developed by the faculty member's supervisor in concert with the faculty member and shall be written. The PIP shall address the deficiencies that caused the overall unsatisfactory rating and identify specific performance goals for the following academic year. The PIP shall outline the problem areas and the actions needed to resolve the problems. It shall be specific enough that it is possible to determine objectively whether the faculty member has met the goals. The goals shall be consistent with performance expectations for other faculty members in similar classifications within the department/unit. If there are no other faculty members in similar classifications within the department/unit, the goals shall be consistent with performance expectations for other faculty members in similar classifications in a comparable department/unit. The PIP must be developed and signed prior to the start of the following semester, excluding summer. If the faculty member and the supervisor are unable to agree on the elements of the PIP the dean or for non-departmental units the Vice President over the unit shall make the final determination on the elements of the PIP. The PIP will require at least four periodic meetings between the faculty member and the Evaluator to review the faculty member's progress. At each meeting, the faculty member shall be apprised in writing of progress toward the goals in the PIP.

(2) The first periodic meeting shall take place no later than three months after the issuance of the PIP. The second periodic meeting shall take place no earlier than six months after the issuance of the performance improvement plan.

(3) During the second and subsequent periodic meetings between the faculty member and the Evaluator, if the faculty member's progress on the PIP is unsatisfactory, the faculty member's contract may be curtailed in accordance with Section 8.6(f) below. However, such a decision shall not be made for a Teaching Track faculty member until she or he has taught at least one complete course, for which she or he has received a teaching evaluation, since the start of the improvement plan.

(4) In the next annual performance evaluation, the faculty member's Evaluator shall review his or her progress in successfully fulfilling the PIP. If the faculty member has met the specified performance goals, the probation shall be lifted and a one or two-year contract extension be granted, depending on the contract type, thereby restoring the faculty member to a full two or four-year multi-year contract cycle. No additional penalties shall attach to the faculty member's appointment as a result of the probationary term.

(5) Curtailment of Appointment. At the end of the probationary year, if the faculty member receives a less than "Meets FSU's High Expectations" on the annual performance evaluation summary form, or is found to not be making satisfactory progress on the PIP at the

second or later periodic meeting according to Section 18.6(d)(3) above, the appointment may be curtailed. Upon receipt by the faculty member of written notice of such curtailment, the length of the remaining contract is reduced to a time period equal to the length of notice to which the faculty member would be entitled according to Section 12.2 if they were not on an MYA.

(6) In the case of early curtailment of an MYA, the faculty member may, within 30 days, request that the decision of the Evaluator be reviewed by a PIP Review Committee. Both the Evaluator and the faculty member may submit any relevant materials to the PIP Review Committee. This committee shall be comprised of three (3) members, one appointed from the faculty member's department/unit by the dean of the college (or for non-departmental units by the Vice President over the unit), one appointed by the UFF, and one appointed by the Vice President for Faculty Development and Advancement. Neither the faculty member's Evaluator nor the department chair (or unit director, in instances where there is no chair) may be a member of the PIP Review Committee. Recommendations from each member of the committee will be forwarded to the President via the office of Human Resources, along with the recommendation of the Evaluator.

(d) Nothing in Section 8.6 Fixed-term Multi-Year Appointments is intended to prevent the Board from applying disciplinary action in accordance with Article 16 Disciplinary Action and Job Abandonment at any time during a fixed-term MYA.

(e) Nothing in Section 8.6 Fixed-term Multi-Year Appointments is intended to diminish the faculty member's rights to notice of non-reappointment as specified in Article 12 Non-Reappointment.

(f) Faculty members on MYAs funded through contracts and grants may have their appointments curtailed should funding become unavailable in the contract or grant from which the faculty member's salary is funded. The early curtailment shall be effective on the same date that the funding ceases on the contract or grant. In cases where the granting agency reduces or redirects funding, early curtailment of the MYA shall not occur prior to the date funding is reduced or redirected. Early curtailment of the MYA shall be effective only after decisions have been made for accommodating the contract or grant changes. In instances where curtailed funding becomes available again and is not otherwise redirected, the faculty member shall be reinstated at the same position classification she or he held at the time of the curtailment, as long as no more than one year has elapsed since the curtailment of the faculty member's previous MYA.

(g) When an early curtailment of an MYA is due to funding changes by a granting agency, the University may provide "bridge" funding from an alternative source for a specified amount of time. Any such agreement between the University and the faculty member shall be in writing and shall not grant rights to continued funding from the alternative source beyond the specified amount of time.

(h) An MYA shall be granted to a faculty member at the time of initial appointment to a classification that carries an MYA.

(i) Reclassification from current to new job classifications as shown in Tables 1-3 of **"Specialized (Non-Tenure-Track) Faculty Reclassification Process, Attachment C"** shall be based upon a review of current specialized faculty members' disciplinary vitae and the three most recent annual evaluations.

(j) Reclassifications shall normally be lateral, and will not imply any change in salary. If a reclassification results in placement of the faculty member into a lower rank, the time counted toward promotion shall begin at the time that the faculty member is reclassified. In the case of a lateral reclassification, time in the previous rank shall count towards promotion. In no case will a faculty member be reclassified to a higher rank without going through a promotion process as specified in Article 14 and Appendix J.

(k) A faculty member may reject the reclassification decision and thereby remain in her or his current job classification but without opportunity for promotion or an MYA, notwithstanding any other provisions of the CBA. Such faculty members may request to be considered for reclassification to a Specialized Faculty position at a later date. Granting such consideration shall be a discretionary matter for the Board, but if such consideration is given, the rules of Section 8.6(a)-(i) shall apply.

(l) Attachments C (Reclassification Process), D (Faculty Title Change Action), and E (Revised and New Classification Specifications) of the **"Specialized (Non-Tenure-Track) Faculty Reclassification Process"** MOA are intended to supplement this Section 8.6 Fixed-term Multi-Year Appointments.

Article 9
ASSIGNMENT OF RESPONSIBILITIES

9.1 Policy.
(a) The Board and the UFF agree that the assignment of responsibilities to faculty members is one of the mechanisms by which the University establishes its priorities, carries out its mission, and creates opportunities to increase the quality and integrity of its academic programs and enhance its reputation and stature as a major research university.

(b) The professional obligation of faculty members (teaching, scholarship/creative activities, service, or other assigned duties) is comprised of both scheduled and nonscheduled activities.

(c) The Board and the UFF recognize that it is a part of the professional responsibility of faculty members to carry out their duties in an appropriate manner and place. For example, while instructional activities, office hours, and other duties and responsibilities may be required to be performed at a specific time and place, non-scheduled activities are more appropriately performed in a manner and place determined by the faculty member.

(d) Each faculty member should be given assignments that are fair and reasonable and provide an equitable opportunity for development and advancement in relation to other faculty in the same department/unit

(e) The Board shall make a reasonable and good faith effort, consistent with the other provisions of this Agreement, to provide faculty members with the necessary facilities and resources for carrying out their assigned duties and responsibilities.

9.2   Considerations in Assignment.
    (a) The Board and the UFF recognize that, while the Legislature has described the minimum full academic assignment in terms of twelve (12) contact hours of instruction or equivalent research and service, the professional obligation undertaken by a faculty member will ordinarily be broader than that minimum and is not easily quantifiable.

    (b) The University has the right, in making assignments, to determine the types of duties and responsibilities that comprise the professional obligation and to determine the mix or relative proportion of effort a faculty member may be required to expend on the various components of the obligation.

    (c) Furthermore, the University properly has the obligation constantly to monitor and review the size and number of classes and other instructional activities, such as laboratories, field experiences, and internships, to consolidate inappropriately small offerings, and to reduce inappropriately large classes.

    (d) The chair shall provide the faculty member with the opportunity to consult about the course schedule and shall make a good faith effort to accommodate a faculty member's teaching preferences to the extent practicable.

    (e) In the case of any contemplated change in the faculty member's assigned allocations for teaching, research/scholarship/creative activity, and service, the chair shall offer the faculty member the opportunity to discuss any such contemplated change and how it alters the Board's expectations of the faculty member's performance in each of the three areas.

    (f) In making assignments, the Board or designees shall also be guided by the following considerations:
        (1) the needs of the program or department/unit;
        (2) the faculty member's qualifications and experiences, including professional growth and development and preferences;
        (3) the character of the assignment, including but not limited to
            a. the number of hours of instruction,

b. the number of distinct preparations required, and the amount required, including the amount of preparation that is new for that faculty member,

c. whether the faculty member has taught the course in the past,

d. the expected number of students enrolled in the course and the time required by the course,

e. whether travel to another location is required,

f. the faculty member's assignments in other semesters,

g. the terms and conditions of a contract or grant from which the faculty member is compensated,

h. the use of instructional technology,

i. the availability and adequacy of materials and equipment, secretarial services, student assistants, and other support services needed to perform the assignments,

j. any changes which have been made in the assignment, including those which may have resulted from previous evaluations of the faculty member,

k. the distribution of day, evening, and weekend courses;

l. the number of hours between the beginning of the first assignment and the end of the last assignment in any one day (normally a maximum of 8 hours),

m. the number of hours between the end of the last assignment on one day and the beginning of the first assignment for the next day (normally at least 12 hours),

n. the degree of individual attention that must be given to students by the faculty member, for grading, conferences, etc.,

o. whether the course is elective or required for students,

p. special assessment and reporting requirements, such as for SMALC and SACS outcomes; and

(4) whether the assignment provides an equitable opportunity, in relation to other faculty members in the same department/unit, the opportunity to fulfill applicable criteria for tenure, promotion, and merit salary increases, and for Salary Plan for Professors (SPP) salary increases if eligible.

(g) The faculty of each department/unit is encouraged to develop guidelines for the distribution of teaching assignments, possibly based on a formula in which points are assigned to various factors affecting the teaching effort. Such guidelines shall be approved by at least a majority of the faculty members in the department/unit, subject to the decision-making procedures defined by the bylaws of the department/unit, but shall be a separate document from the bylaws.

9.3 Annual Assignment.

(a) Communication of Assignment. Faculty members shall be apprised in print or electronically, at the beginning of their employment and prior to the beginning of each academic year of employment thereafter, of the duties assigned in teaching, research and other creative activities, public service, and of any other specific duties assigned for that year.

(1) Except for an assignment made at the beginning of a faculty member's employment,

the assigner shall notify the faculty member well in advance of making the final assignment. The assignment shall be communicated to faculty members at least eight (8) weeks in advance of its starting date, if practicable. For continuing faculty members, the assignment of responsibilities shall be provided no later than May 1, and changes shall be according to Section 9.3(b), below. New faculty members shall be informed of assigned duties as soon as practicable.

(2) After the faculty member has been notified of and has been provided the opportunity to discuss the assignment, the assigner shall forward the AOR for acknowledgement by the faculty member and approval by the dean or, if the assigner is a dean, for approval by the Vice President for Faculty Development and Advancement. The assigner shall receive from the dean or the Vice President for Faculty Development and Advancement printed or electronic notification within 60 days of receipt, either indicating approval or directing a change in the assignment.

(4) The faculty member's acknowledgement of the assignment certifies that the faculty member has been given an opportunity to discuss the assignment, and that the final assignment has been communicated. All faculty members shall acknowledge receipt of their assignment. Those who want to dispute an assignment should refer to the procedures in Appendix H of this Agreement.

(5) The date of receipt of the assignment by a faculty member shall be the date that the faculty member acknowledges the AOR. If the faculty member refuses or otherwise fails to acknowledge the form within 14 days of receipt, the date shall be established by sending a copy of the form to the faculty member by certified mail with return receipt, or by signature of a third-party witness.

(b) Instructional Assignment. The period of an instructional assignment during an academic year shall not exceed an average of seventy-five (75) days per semester and the period for testing, advisement, and other scheduled assignments shall not exceed an average of ten (10) days per semester. Within each semester, activities referred to above shall be scheduled during contiguous weeks with the exception of spring break, if any. Determination of the level of effort (FTE) required to perform a given teaching assignment shall take into consideration the factors listed in 9.2 and the principle of equity relative to the assignments of other faculty members in the same department/unit.

(c) Change in Assignment.

(1) If it should become necessary to make changes in a faculty member's assignment, the person responsible for making the change shall notify the faculty member as soon as practicable prior to making such change and shall document and communicate the changed assignment as specified in 9.3 (a) above.

(2) If a change in assignment results in needing to move University property, the Board shall provide assistance in such a move and shall notify the faculty member of the time of the move. For a substantial amount of property such as a lab or studio the Board shall provide at least one (1) month advance notice.

(3) The Board shall make a reasonable and good faith effort not to change the same

faculty member's teaching assignment fewer than four (4) weeks prior to the first class session in two consecutive academic years.

(4) If a faculty member has been assigned or reassigned a course fewer than four (4) weeks prior to the first class session, such circumstances shall be taken into consideration when reviewing student evaluations of the course and determining how much weight to give them, if any.

(5) A change in assignment shall not be made as a means of retaliatory action. However, the Board may change a faculty member's assignment as a consequence of disciplinary action taken in accordance with Article 16 Disciplinary Action and Job Abandonment.

(d) Equitable Opportunity.

(1) Each faculty member shall be given assignments that provide equitable opportunities, in relation to other faculty members in the same department/unit, to meet the required criteria for promotion, tenure, and merit salary increases, and for Salary Plan for Professors (SPP) salary increases if eligible.

(2) For the purpose of applying this principle to promotion, assignments shall be considered over the entire period since the original appointment or since the last promotion, not solely over the period of a single annual assignment. The period under consideration at the University shall not be less than four years. The faculty member's annual assignment shall be included in the promotion file.

(3) For the purpose of applying this principle to tenure, assignments shall be considered over the entire probationary period and not solely over the period of a single annual assignment. The faculty member's annual assignments shall be included in the tenure file. If an arbitrator determines that the faculty member was not provided an "equitable opportunity" as described in this section, the arbitrator may award additional employment requiring the University to provide the "equitable opportunity" as described herein. The arbitrator also may retain jurisdiction for purposes of determining whether the ensuing assignment provides such "equitable opportunity."

(4) If it is determined that a faculty member has not received assignments that provide equitable opportunities to meet the required criteria for any of the advancements listed in 9.3(d), then the faculty member must receive a timely appropriate adjustment in the faculty member's assignment that corrects the inequity. The fact that the faculty member was not provided equitable opportunity shall also be taken into account when determining merit salary increases.

(e) Review. The Assignment of Responsibilities (AOR) shall be reviewed by the administrative officer responsible for review of the annual performance evaluation, specified in 10.5(c). The reviewer will normally be the dean of the college or school in which the faculty member holds the faculty position. When the dean of a school or college is the assigner, the Assignment of Responsibilities shall be reviewed by the Vice President for Faculty Development and Advancement. The reviewer will check that the AOR is submitted for review in a timely fashion and contains a level of detail appropriate for forming the basis for the annual performance evaluation.

9.4   Resolution of Assignment Disputes

(a) The faculty member shall be granted promptly, upon written request, a conference with the person responsible for making the assignment (the assigner) to express concerns regarding the considerations listed in subsection 9.2.

(b) If the conference with the assigner does not resolve the faculty member's concerns, the faculty member shall promptly be granted, upon written request, an opportunity to discuss those concerns with an administrator at the next higher level. If the faculty member's concerns are not resolved, the faculty member may address the matter through the expedited Neutral Umpire procedure described in Appendix "H" of this Agreement. The faculty member shall perform the assignment until final resolution of the matter as prescribed in this Agreement, unless the assignment violates this Agreement, University policies, or applicable law.

(c) No faculty member's assignment shall be imposed arbitrarily or unreasonably. For the purpose of applying this principle to assignments, assignments shall be deemed arbitrary or unreasonable if one or more of the following applies:

(1) The assignment was made without providing the faculty member the opportunity to consult about the assignment.

(2) After consulting with the faculty member, the Board or designees did not make a fair and reasonable attempt to accommodate the faculty member's circumstances, including allowing reasonable time for research for those faculty members with research assignments. In this regard, the parties recognize the following:

a. Teaching assignments are driven primarily by the program and curricular needs of the students in the programs in the department. The teaching preferences and desires of the faculty members are secondary to these program and curricular needs.

b. Not all circumstances can be accommodated, and that inability to accommodate does not in and of itself represent an arbitrary or unreasonable assignment.

(3) The time between the beginning of the first assignment and the end of the last assignment in any one day exceeds eight (8) hours, unless the faculty member has agreed to such an arrangement or there is no practicable alternative.

(4) The time between the end of the last assignment on one day and the beginning of the first assignment for the next day is less than twelve (12) hours, unless the faculty member has agreed to such an arrangement or there is no practicable alternative.

(5) If, in relation to other faculty members in the same department, the assignment does not provide an equitable opportunity to meet the required criteria for promotion, tenure, awards, and merit salary increases, or there has been no provision for a timely appropriate adjustment that corrects the inequity.

(d) If a faculty member believes that the assignment is arbitrary or unreasonable, the faculty member should proceed to address the matter through the procedures in Appendix "H" of this Agreement, which shall be the exclusive method for resolving such disputes. Other claims of alleged violations of the Agreement with respect to faculty member assignments are subject to the provisions of Article 20, Grievance Procedure and Arbitration.

9.5   Summer Assignment.
    (a) The summer instructional assignment, like that for the academic year, includes the normal activities related to such an assignment as defined by the department/unit and the nature of the course, such as course preparation, minor curriculum development, lectures, evaluation of student efforts, consultations and conferences with students, and minor committee activities.

    (b) When a summer instructional appointment immediately follows the academic year appointment, the faculty member may be assigned reasonable and necessary non-instructional duties related to the summer instructional appointment prior to the conclusion of the academic year appointment.

9.6   Place of Employment.
    (a) Principal. Each faculty member shall be assigned one principal place of employment, as stated on the University employment contract. Where possible, a faculty member shall be given at least nine (9) months notice of a change in principal place of employment. The faculty member shall be granted, upon written request, a conference with the person responsible for making the change to express concerns regarding such change, including concerns regarding considerations in assignment as described in Section 9.2 above. Voluntary changes and available new positions within the department shall be considered prior to involuntary changes, if practicable.

    (b) Secondary. Each faculty member, where possible, shall be given at least ninety (90) days written notice of assignment to a secondary place of employment more than fifteen (15) miles from the faculty member's principal place of employment. The faculty member shall be granted, upon written request, a conference with the person responsible for making the change to express concerns regarding such change. If the assignment to a secondary place of employment is made within a regular full-time appointment, the assigner is encouraged to make an appropriate adjustment in the assignment in recognition of time spent traveling to a secondary place of employment. Necessary travel expenses, including overnight lodging and meals, for all assignments not at the faculty member's principal place of employment shall be paid at the State rate and in accordance with the applicable provisions of State law.

9.7   Teaching Schedule. Teaching schedules should be established, if practicable, so that the time between the beginning of the first assignment and the end of the last for any one day does not exceed eight (8) hours.

9.8   Equipment.
    (a) The Board shall make a reasonable and good-faith effort to provide and maintain an adequate inventory of technologically current equipment necessary to carry out assigned duties,

and shall make a reasonable and good faith effort to obtain funding to provide for the replacement of obsolete equipment.

(b) When equipment is required for classes, laboratories, or studios, or at recitals, practica, or other such performances, exhibitions or instructional activities, it is desirable that the Board provide sufficient and adequate equipment to accommodate the students assigned in them. If the Board does not provide sufficient and adequate equipment, such circumstances shall be taken into consideration in reviewing student evaluations of the course and determining how much weight to give them, if any.

9.9   Schedule of Assigned Duties. Scheduled hours for all faculty members shall not normally exceed forty (40) hours per week. Time shall be allowed within the normal working day for research, teaching, or other activities required of the faculty member, when a part of the assigned duties. The assigner is encouraged to make appropriate reductions or adjustments in the number of hours scheduled in recognition of evening, night, and weekend assignments, and for periods when a faculty member is on call. Evenings, nights, and weekends when a faculty member is on call shall be considered in making other assignments. See Section 17.5 regarding schedule adjustment for holiday assignment.

9.10   Specialized Faculty. The Specialized Faculty comprises several tracks, each of which has three ranks.
   (a) The Specialized Faculty tracks are as follows:
      (1) Teaching
          Teaching Faculty I (position code 9060)
          Teaching Faculty II (position code 9061)
          Teaching Faculty III (position code 9062)
      (2) Instructional Support
          Instructional Specialist I (position code 9070)
          Instructional Specialist II (position code 9071)
          Instructional Specialist III (position code 9072)
      (3) Research
          Research Faculty I (position code 9080)
          Research Faculty II (position code 9081)
          Research Faculty III (position code 9082)
      (4) Research Support
          Assistant in Research (position code 9168)
          Associate in Research (position code 9167)
          Senior Research Associate (position code 9165)
       (5) Library or Information Specialties
          Assistant University Librarian (position code 9055)
          Associate University Librarian (position code 9054)
          University Librarian (position code 9053)

(6) Curator Specialties
Assistant Curator (position code 9152)
Associate Curator (position code 9151)
Curator (position code 9150)

(b) Restrictions on Duty Assignments. The following restrictions on percent assignments of responsibility apply to positions in these tracks:

(1) A full-time faculty member in the Teaching track shall normally be assigned not less than 75% teaching responsibility and not more than 5% research responsibility, averaged over any academic year, except as specified for certain administrative codes in Section 9.10(b)(6).

(2) A full-time faculty member in the Instructional Support track shall normally be assigned not less than 75% service responsibility in the area of instructional support, and not more than 5% research responsibility, averaged over any academic year, except as specified for certain administrative codes in Section 9.10(b)(6).

(3) A full-time faculty member in the Research track shall normally be assigned not less than 75% research responsibility, and not more than 5% teaching responsibility, averaged over any academic year, except as specified for certain administrative codes in Section 9.10(b)(6). Directed Individual Studies (DIS) may be considered part of the research assignment for a full-time faculty member in the Research track. Only under the following combination of circumstances, and for one semester per emergency situation, a faculty member in the Research track may be given a temporary teaching assignment to teach a single course:

a. The course is a specialized graduate level course required for degree-seeking students, that is regularly offered and is not a "special topics," "selected topics," or "seminar" course;

b. There is a bona fide emergency, in which the faculty member assigned to teach a course becomes incapacitated or otherwise becomes unable to teach the course, either while the course is already in progress or so near the start of the term that there are students enrolled in the course and no workable alternative way of teaching the course to those students can be found;

c. The faculty member is not willing to perform the teaching assignment as a dual compensation appointment under Section 8.5(c), and;

d. There is no one else qualified to teach the course, or for those who are qualified, they already have a maximum teaching assignment for the semester that cannot be adjusted to meet the need of teaching the course in question and they are unwilling to teach the course as an overload on a dual compensation appointment.

(4) A full-time faculty member in the Research Support track shall normally be assigned not less than 95% combined responsibility in research and service in support of research, and not more than 5% teaching responsibility, averaged over any academic year, except as specified for certain administrative codes in Section 9.10(b)(6) below.

(5) "Abnormal assignments" are those that provide for unique opportunities that benefit the University. Such assignment requests shall be reviewed by the President or Provost within thirty (30) days, and if approved, reported within 10 days to the Director of Human Resources and the UFF.

(6) If a faculty member is assigned one of the in-unit administrative codes, some portion of the minimum assignment in the area of specialization required by Sections 9.10(b)(1)-(4) above may be replaced by a service assignment.

(7) For part-time positions, the percentages in Sections 9.10(b)(1)-(4) above shall be pro-rated, relative to the total appointment.

(8) Sections 9.10(b)(1)-(4) only apply to the first 100% FTE appointment. They shall not prevent a faculty member from accepting a supplemental dual compensation appointment outside of the area of specialization.

(9) A faculty member in a Specialized Faculty position may not hold a concurrent split appointment between multiple tracks.

(10) Specialized faculty members may serve on doctoral supervisory committees in a department if approved by the faculty of the department for doctoral supervision, and if they meet Faculty Senate requirements. In regard to directing doctoral theses, a specialized faculty member may serve only as a co-director or as a non-directing member of the committee, and another co-director must be a member of the tenure-track or tenured faculty (Assistant, Associate, Full Professor or Eminent Scholar). The specialized faculty member must also be approved by the chair of the department for service on the specific committee. For any doctoral committee, the director or at least one co-director must be a member of the tenure-track or tenured faculty (Assistant, Associate, Full Professor or Eminent Scholar) of the department/unit in which the degree is to be granted. If the doctoral degree is sought in an interdisciplinary area of study, the director or at least one co-director must be a tenure-track or a tenured faculty member in a department/unit related to the area of interdisciplinary study. However, those who are not members of the tenure-track faculty who have served as director of an active doctoral dissertation committee between the dates of July 1, 2008 and July 1, 2013 shall remain eligible to direct doctoral theses and dissertations.

9.11   Assigned Development/Use of Instructional Technology.

(a) "Instructional technology material" includes any manner of physical or virtual media delivered synchronously or asynchronously includes, but is not limited to, images, video, online content, structures, audio materials, computer programs, virtualization software, computer assisted instructional materials, programmed instructional materials, and combinations of the above materials, which are prepared or produced in whole or in part by a faculty member for the purpose of assisting or enhancing instruction.

(b) The parties recognize the increasing development and use of technology may improve teaching and learning and may enhance the fundamental relationship between faculty member and student. This technology may be used in the context of distance learning or to augment classroom instruction. Furthermore, the parties recognize that this technology should be used to the maximum mutual benefit of the University and the faculty member.

(c) The parties recognize that faculty effort spent in the development of instructional technology, including but not limited to distance learning materials, and in providing instruction

Article 9
ASSIGNMENT OF RESPONSIBILITIES

in this manner is appreciably greater than that associated with a traditional course. Therefore, when the University assigns faculty members to develop or provide instruction through the use of instructional technology, the University shall:

(1) Make training and development resources available to faculty members.

(2) Provide clerical, technical, and library support in conjunction with the assigned use of instructional technology.

(3) Account for the additional effort required to develop, revise, and offer a course using instructional technology in the annual duty assignment, or provide additional compensation pursuant to Section 8.5(b) Summer Appointments or 8.5(c) Dual Compensation Appointments. More specifically, for distance learning courses:

a. If a faculty member is assigned responsibility for development of a new distance learning course, including the content and the associated instructional technology materials, the duty assignments prior to the first offering of the course shall, upon approval of the assigner, reflect an appropriate level of effort for course development equivalent to teaching a regular three (3) credit hour course for up to two semesters, or the faculty member shall receive equivalent extra compensation.

b. If a faculty member is assigned responsibility for a major revision of an existing distance learning course, including the content and the associated instructional technology materials, the duty assignment for the term in which the revision is done shall reflect a level of effort for course revision equivalent to teaching a regular three (3) credit hour course for one semester, or the faculty member shall receive equivalent extra compensation.

c. If a faculty member is assigned responsibility for teaching a distance learning course the duty assignment shall allow for the necessary additional individual communications with distance learning students.

d. If a faculty member is assigned both conventional classroom delivery and distance delivery of a course in the same semester, the duty assignment shall reflect the classroom and distance offerings as separate courses.

(d) The faculty member shall not make use of appreciable University support in the creation or revision of instructional technology materials unless the University approves such use in advance and in writing.

(e) Releases for Instructional Technology Materials.

(1) Provisions governing the intellectual property rights of faculty members and releases to be obtained when the University has an interest in instructional technology are contained in Article 18. Consistent with such provisions and prior to the use by the faculty member of the instructional technology materials described in Section 9.11(a), above, releases shall be obtained from persons appearing in, or giving financial or creative support to their development or use, and the faculty member shall certify that such development or use does not infringe upon any existing copyright or other legal right. The faculty member shall be liable to the University for judgments resulting from such infringements.

(2) The University shall assist the faculty member in obtaining releases regarding

instructional technology materials when:

    a. the University has asserted an interest in such materials; or

    b. the University has assigned the faculty member to develop such materials.

Article 10
PERFORMANCE EVALUATIONS

10.1   Purpose and Scope of Evaluation. The basic purpose of faculty evaluation is to recognize, reward, and improve faculty performance in the functions of teaching, research, service, and administrative and related duties that may be assigned.

10.2   Sources and Methods for Evaluation. Evaluations shall be based only upon assigned duties, and shall carefully consider the nature of the assignments and quality of the performance. Evaluations shall be based upon the assignments of responsibility, as described in Article 9, and any dual compensation appointments, if applicable, for the period under evaluation, and shall take into account the proportions, duties and nature of the assignments.

    (a) All evaluations shall be performed during the spring semester (with the exception of Sustained Performance Evaluations which may for 2012 be performed in the fall term) and shall take into account performance of assigned duties over a period consistent with approved department criteria and may include multiple years. For faculty members who have been employed at the University less than that period, the annual evaluation shall take into account their performance since the start of employment at the University.

    (b) An evaluation may only be changed through the appeal process as outlined in the provisions of this article or through other provisions of the Agreement.

    (c) The faculty of each department/unit shall develop and maintain specific written criteria and procedures by which to evaluate faculty members consistent with the criteria specified in this Article and subject to the approval of the unit's dean. These criteria and procedures shall be the sole basis upon which faculty performance is measured.

    (d) Development Process for Criteria and Procedures. If criteria and procedures for evaluating faculty performance are not on file, they shall be developed. If such criteria and procedures are already on file, the faculty of the department/unit shall review and revise them after ratification of this Agreement.

    (1) The department/unit administrator shall discuss with the department/unit faculty members who are to participate in the development or revision process the existing criteria and procedures of the department/unit, the mission and goals of the department/unit and the University, the provisions of the BOT-UFF Collective Bargaining Agreement, and relevant state law. A copy of the BOT-UFF Collective Bargaining Agreement and the relevant portions of state law shall be provided to each department/unit at the outset of the process.

    (2) These criteria and procedures, and any revisions thereof, shall be recommended by a

secret ballot vote of a majority of the faculty members in the department/unit.

(e) These criteria and procedures shall

(1) Be consistent with the criteria and procedures specified in this Article and with all the other provisions of this Agreement.

(2) Satisfy all provisions of Article 23 with regard to department/unit criteria and evaluative procedures for the distribution of merit-based salary increases.

(3) Be adaptable to various assigned duties, so that all faculty have an equal opportunity to earn favorable performance evaluations. The criteria must provide that the FTE allocated to each part of the faculty member's annual assignment shall be used to weight the performance of each part for determination of the overall assessment of performance/merit.

(4) Take into consideration the department's mission and reasonable expectations for different classifications/ranks, experience, and stages of career.

(5) Provide for a peer review component in the annual evaluation.

(6) Specify a new effective date of January 1, 2013.

(7) Be detailed enough that any reasonable faculty member can understand what performance is required to earn each performance evaluation rating.

(8) Ensure that faculty members on approved leave are not penalized in the evaluation process.

(f) The criteria and procedures shall be periodically reviewed by the faculty for consistency, revised as appropriate, and subjected to a reaffirmation ballot whenever a change is made to this Article. Subsequent revisions may be initiated by a majority vote of at least a quorum of the faculty members subject to evaluation or upon the initiative of the department/unit administrator.

(g) Departments/units are encouraged to exchange and discuss drafts of their faculty evaluation criteria and procedures during the formulation and revision processes.

(h) Approval Process.

(1) The University President or representative shall review the proposed criteria and procedures or revisions thereof to ensure that they comply with the provisions of this Article. The President or representative shall notify the department/unit of his or her approval or non-approval within sixty (60) days of receipt, if practicable. However, final notification shall occur no later than ninety (90) days after receipt. In the case of a non-approval, the notification will provide a written statement of reasons.

(2) In the case of non-approval, the department/unit has ninety (90) days after notification to revise and resubmit the proposal, and the President or representative shall review it within sixty (60) days of receipt and notify the department of approval or non-approval, and in the case of non-approval, provide a written statement of reasons. In the event that the next version is also not approved, the criteria shall be forwarded to the Vice President for Faculty Development and Advancement who will resolve any discrepancies and the criteria and procedures shall be imposed.

(i) Approved or imposed faculty evaluation criteria and procedures, and revisions thereof, and any related recommendations shall be kept on file in the department/unit and college offices, in the Office of Faculty Development and Advancement, and posted on the department/unit and college/unit websites. Faculty members in each department/unit shall be provided a copy of that department's/unit's current faculty evaluation criteria and procedures at the start of the spring semester.

(j) No merit or market equity salary increases shall be provided to a department/unit until its faculty evaluation criteria and procedures have been approved by the University President or representative.

(k) No faculty member shall be evaluated according to new criteria and procedures prior to the President or representative's final approval of these criteria and procedures or until they are imposed by the Vice President for Faculty Development and Advancement.

(l) No evaluations shall require a forced or pre-specified distribution of ratings.

10.3 Annual Evaluations. Annual performance evaluations shall be based upon the assignments of responsibility, as described in Article 9, for the period under evaluation, and shall take into account the proportions, duties and nature of the assignments. The faculty member's history of annual evaluations shall be considered in recommendations and final decisions on promotions (except to Associate Professor) and appointment and non-reappointment.

(a) Sources for Annual Evaluations. In preparing the annual evaluation, the person(s) responsible for evaluating the faculty member may consider, in light of the department/unit's faculty evaluation criteria, pertinent information from the following sources: immediate supervisor, peers, students, faculty member/self, other University officials who have responsibility for supervision of the faculty member, and individuals to whom the faculty member may be responsible in the course of a service assignment, including public school officials when a faculty member has a service assignment to the public schools.

(b) Teaching effectiveness. Includes effectiveness in presenting knowledge, information, and ideas by means or methods such as lecture, discussion, assignment and recitation, demonstration, laboratory exercise, practical experience, and direct consultation with students.

(1) The evaluation shall include consideration of effectiveness in imparting knowledge and skills, and effectiveness in stimulating students' critical thinking and/or creative abilities, the development or revision of curriculum and course structure, and adherence to accepted standards of professional behavior in meeting responsibilities to students.

(2) The evaluation shall include consideration of class size format, preparation time, whether the course is required or elective, availability of assistance, and other University teaching duties, such as advising, counseling, supervision of interns, or duties described in a Position Description, if any, of the position held by the faculty member.

(3) The teaching evaluation must take into account any relevant materials submitted by the faculty member. Examples of such materials include class notes, syllabi, student exams and

assignments, supplementary material and peer evaluations of teaching. The teaching evaluation may not be based primarily on student perceptions when additional information has been made available to the evaluator.

(4) Observation/Visitation.

a.   The faculty member, if assigned teaching duties, shall be notified at least two (2) weeks in advance of the date, time, and place of any direct classroom observation or visitation (including visitation or monitoring of a course website) made in connection with the faculty member's annual evaluation. If the faculty member determines that this date is not appropriate, because of the scheduled class activities, the faculty member and the person(s) responsible for performing the observation or visitation will mutually agree upon an alternate date.

b.   Upon request, a faculty member is entitled to an evaluation of teaching based on direct observation or visitation by one or more peers.

c.   Whenever a person conducts a classroom visit for the purpose of evaluation, a report of his/her observations must be submitted to the faculty member within ten (10) working days of the observation. Otherwise, nothing from the visit may be used in the evaluation process.

i.   The report must suggest corrective actions for any shortcoming that is identified.

ii.   No corrective actions that impinge upon academic freedom may be suggested.

d.   A faculty member who challenges an observation report may choose a colleague to observe his or her class and submit a report. The colleague may be from the same department/unit, from a department/unit with a compatible discipline, a retired colleague, or a colleague in the discipline from another university. Such a report shall be given equal consideration with other reports of classroom visitation.

(c) Contribution to the discovery of new knowledge.   Includes development of new educational techniques, and other forms of creative activity.

(1) Evidence of research and other creative activity shall include, but not be limited to, published books, chapters in books, articles in refereed and un-refereed professional journals, musical compositions, exhibits of paintings and sculpture, works of performance art, papers presented at meetings of professional societies, reviews, and research and creative activity that has not yet resulted in publication, display, or performance.

(2) The evaluation shall include consideration of the faculty member's productivity, including the quality and quantity of the faculty member's research and other creative programs and contributions during the period under evaluation. The evaluation of quality shall include consideration of recognitions by the academic or professional community.

(d) Service. Evaluation of service shall include consideration of contributions to:

(1) the orderly and effective functioning of the faculty member's academic unit (program, department, school, college) and/or the total University, including participation in regular departmental or college meetings;

(2) the University community, including participation in the governance processes of the institution through significant service on University committees and councils, in UFF activities,

and in Faculty Senate activities;

(3) the local, state, regional and national communities, and scholarly and professional associations, including participation in professional meetings, symposia, conferences, workshops, service on local, state, and national governmental boards, agencies and commissions; and service to public or private schools;

(4) other assigned University duties, such as academic administration, of the position held by the faculty member. Evaluations for department chairs should consider responsibilities of the chair such as departmental planning and goal setting, assignment of work responsibilities and resources, fiscal responsibilities, recruitment and hiring, mentoring, evaluation of faculty, handling of personnel issues involving faculty and staff, academic program responsibilities, implementation of University policy, and communication both within the department and with administrators regarding the department;

(5) such other responsibilities as may be appropriate to the assignment.

(e) These criteria may be elaborated, augmented, and refined by recommendation of the faculty of the department/unit, as provided in this Article.

(f) Methods for Annual Performance Evaluations

(1) Evaluator. The evaluator will normally be the administrator of the department/ unit in which the faculty member holds an appointment at the time the evaluation is performed. Faculty members holding concurrent appointments in more than one department/unit shall be evaluated by the administrators of each unit in which they hold an appointment. Faculty members earning or holding tenure in a unit in which they do not hold an appointment shall also be evaluated by the administrator of the unit in which they are earning or hold tenure.

a. Department/unit administrators who are faculty members shall be evaluated by their respective deans.

b. Each evaluator shall be familiar with the provisions of this Agreement, any applicable Florida Statues and Board policies, and the department/unit criteria and procedures specified by this Article for the annual evaluation of the faculty.

(2) The performance of faculty members, other than those who have received notice of non-reappointment under Article 12 or are not entitled to receive notice of non-reappointment under Article 12, shall be evaluated. The evaluation shall be consistent with the criteria specified in Section 10.2.

(3) Evidence of Performance Report. The administrator responsible for the annual evaluation shall request each member of the faculty to submit to him or her, annually, a report of Evidence of Performance in teaching, research or creative activities, service, and other University duties where appropriate.

a. The Evidence of Performance report (EOP) shall be submitted after the end of each calendar year, and shall cover the preceding calendar year.

b. Each department/unit shall specify in detail the required format and minimal content of the EOP, pursuant to this section.

c. The EOP shall also include any interpretive comments or supporting data that the faculty member deems appropriate in evaluating his or her performance.

d. Any materials required for the EOP that depend on the University administration shall be provided to the faculty member no less than fourteen (14) days prior to the date upon which the Evidence of Performance report is due.

(4) Those persons responsible for supervising and evaluating shall endeavor to assist the person being evaluated in correcting any performance deficiencies reflected in the evaluation.

(5) The Annual Performance Evaluation shall provide for an assessment of performance for each faculty member using the following ratings:

a. Substantially Exceeds FSU's High Expectations
b. Exceeds FSU's High Expectations
c. Meets FSU's High Expectations
d. Official Concern
e. Does Not Meet FSU's High Expectations

10.4   Merit Evaluations.

(a) The determination of meritorious performance for the distribution of funds allocated for merit-based salary increases pursuant to Article 23 shall be according to each department/unit's faculty evaluation criteria and procedures developed pursuant to this section, which must be consistent with the criteria for faculty evaluation specified elsewhere in this Article. All faculty members will be reviewed for merit.

(b) These criteria and procedures may include any refinements of the methods for the distribution of salary increase funds that are permitted by Article 23 and are based on the annual performance evaluation.

(c) Merit distribution criteria:

(1) Must define meritorious performance as "performance that meets or exceeds the expectations for the position classification and department/unit."

(2) May permit, but not mandate, a merit pay award for all members of the department/unit.

(3) Must establish distinctive levels of merit reflecting the differences in performance.

(d) Merit distribution plans are subject to the approval of the department chair (or in non-departmentalized units, the dean). If the chair makes any changes to the merit distribution plan proposed by a faculty evaluation committee, she/he shall report such changes to the faculty evaluation committee, if there is such a body. The original merit distribution plan along with any recommendations by the chair shall be submitted to the dean and the provost. The dean and the provost provide final approval of merit distribution plans. Any changes at this level to the merit distribution plan shall be reported to the chair by the dean's office, and the chair will inform the faculty evaluation committee, if there is such a body.

10.5 Annual Evaluation Reporting Procedures

(a) Evaluation Summary Form. The evaluator shall annually prepare the faculty member's written annual performance evaluation on the Annual Evaluation Summary Form provided in Appendix "F." The completed form and its attachments comprise the annual evaluation report.

(1) This Evaluation Summary Form and its attachments shall be distributed to the faculty member no later than June 15.

(2) Faculty members holding joint appointments in other areas, departments or divisions shall be evaluated concurrently using the same criteria and procedures as other faculty in the department/unit. Each evaluator shall evaluate the faculty member only with respect to principal duties within that department/unit. Such concurrent summaries shall be forwarded to the administrator responsible for review of evaluations for the department/unit as specified in (c) below.

(3) Faculty members eligible for promotion or for tenure (except for Assistant Professors in the years in which they receive second and fourth year reviews) shall be apprised annually in writing of progress towards promotion or tenure in order to provide assistance and counseling in working toward that goal.

(4) All faculty members, including those ineligible for promotion, shall receive a narrative evaluation appended to the Evaluation Summary Form.

(5) The provision on the Annual Evaluation Summary Form under the heading "TEACHING" for certification of Spoken English Competency shall be utilized only:

a. to certify competency following completion of options for remediation specified following an "Official Concern" evaluation in this area given either in the previous annual evaluation or with an original appointment, or

b. to call into question a previous certification of competency.

(6) If "Official Concern" is noted in the Spoken English Competency category, options for remediation shall be in writing with a copy attached to the Annual Evaluation Summary Form.

(7) The evaluation report shall be signed and dated by the person performing the evaluation.

(b) Discussion. After completion of the Annual Evaluation Summary Form, the evaluator shall discuss the Summary with the faculty member concerned.

(1) The faculty member may attach to the Summary any statement he or she desires.

(2) The persons responsible for supervising and evaluating shall endeavor to assist the person being evaluated in correcting any performance deficiencies reflected in the evaluation.

(3) For non-tenured faculty members, in the case of an evaluation rating of "Does Not Meet FSU's High Expectations," the evaluator shall fully document the rating prior to discussion with the faculty member. Non-tenured faculty members whose overall performance is rated "Does Not Meet FSU's High Expectations" in any given year may be placed on a Performance Improvement Plan (PIP). A tenured faculty member whose overall performance is rated "Does Not Meet FSU's High Expectations" in three (3) or more of the previous six (6) evaluations may be placed on a PIP. A PIP shall be developed in one or more areas of assigned duties. The PIP shall be developed by the faculty member's supervisor in concert with the faculty member, and

shall be written. It shall include specific performance goals and timetables to assist the faculty member in achieving at least a "Meets FSU's High Expectations" rating. Specific resources identified in an approved PIP, shall be provided by the department/unit. Examples of recommendations/resources include, but are not limited to: audit a course; participate in a webinar or webcast; work with or observe the work of an outstanding professor; etc. If the faculty member and the supervisor are unable to agree on the elements of the PIP, the dean shall make the final determination on the elements of the PIP. The PIP shall be approved by the President or representative and attached to the Annual Evaluation Summary Form. The supervisor shall meet periodically with the faculty member to review progress toward meeting the performance goals. It is the responsibility of the faculty member to successfully complete the PIP.

(4) After discussion is completed and attachments made, the faculty member will indicate that the evaluation has been reviewed by signing the Annual Evaluation Summary Form and indicating the number of pages attached to it. The required signature of the person being evaluated certifies that the required discussion of the rating has taken place. It does not imply that the person being evaluated has agreed with the rating. Those not agreeing should be referred to the procedure for appealing an Annual Evaluation Summary, in Section 10.7.

(5) A copy of the Annual Evaluation Summary Form and attachments shall be made available to the person being evaluated.

(c) Review. The Annual Evaluation Summary Form and attachments shall be reviewed by the appropriate administrative officer. The reviewer will normally be the dean of the college in which the faculty member holds the faculty position. When the dean of a college is the evaluator, the Annual Evaluation Summary shall be reviewed by the Vice President for Faculty Development and Advancement.

(1) Upon the completion of the discussion with the faculty member, the Annual Evaluation Summary Form and attachments shall be forwarded to the appropriate reviewer.

(2) The reviewer shall sign the Annual Evaluation Summary Form and attachments if he or she agrees with it.

(3) If the reviewer disagrees, he or she may discuss the area of disagreement with the evaluator, at which time two courses of action are available to the reviewer: The reviewer may submit his or her own Evaluation Summary Form and attachments or may revise the original. When the reviewer prepares his or her own Faculty Evaluation Summary, the original Evaluation Summary Form and attachments must be appended to the reviewer's summary.

(d) In the event of the non-renewal of a faculty member at a date other than the end of an academic year, a special report shall be prepared. A special report may also be required when directed by the President, Provost and Academic Vice President, or the Vice President for Faculty Development and Advancement.

10.6   Disposition of the Evaluation Summary Form and attachments.

(a) After the Evaluation Summary Form and attachments have been reviewed by the appropriate reviewer, they shall be filed in the faculty member's official evaluation file. The contents of the faculty evaluation file shall be confidential and shall not be disclosed except to the faculty member evaluated and those whose duties require access.

(b) For faculty holding joint appointments copies of all evaluations shall be filed in the official evaluation file.

(c) When the overall performance is rated "Does Not Meet FSU's High Expectations," a copy of the Evaluation Summary Form and attachments must be forwarded to the Provost and Vice President for Academic Affairs and the President of the University through the Vice President for Faculty Development and Advancement.

10.7 Provision for Appeal

(a) If a faculty member is dissatisfied with an evaluation, including the determination of failure to successfully complete a PIP. Summary, the faculty member may register his or her disagreement in writing.

(b) In addition, if the faculty member is not satisfied with an evaluation, he or she may present his or her request for review in writing to the appropriate reviewer within thirty (30) days after being informed of the evaluation. The reviewer, like the evaluator, shall have complete freedom of action, consistent with this Agreement, in seeking to settle or resolve differences concerning evaluations and presumably his or her efforts will be largely conciliatory. The reviewer shall meet with the faculty member to discuss the request within fifteen (15) days of receipt of the written request for review. Within fifteen (15) days of receipt of the written request, the reviewer shall reach a decision and report it to the faculty member.

(c) If the faculty member is not satisfied with the reviewer's decision, the faculty member may request in writing a review from the Vice President for Faculty Development and Advancement within fifteen (15) days after the reviewer's decision. Within fifteen (15) days of receipt of the written request, the Vice President for Faculty Development and Advancement shall meet with the faculty member to discuss the request. Within fifteen (15) days of receipt of the written request, the Vice President for Faculty Development and Advancement shall reach a decision and report it to the faculty member.

(d) An appeal of the decision of the Vice President for Faculty Development and Advancement may be made to the Provost and Vice President for Academic Affairs. Such a request for review shall be made in writing within fifteen (15) days after the Vice President for Faculty Development and Advancement' decision. Within fifteen (15) days of the receipt of the written request, the Provost and Vice President for Academic Affairs shall reach a decision and report it to the faculty member.

10.8   Sustained Performance Evaluations.

Article 10
PERFORMANCE EVALUATIONS

(a) Tenured faculty members shall receive a sustained performance evaluation once every seven years following the award of tenure or their most recent promotion, whichever is most recent. The purpose of this evaluation is to document sustained performance during the previous six years of assigned duties and to encourage continued professional growth and development.

(b) The sustained performance evaluation program shall provide that:

(1) Only elected faculty members may participate in the development of applicable procedures. Such procedures shall ensure involvement of both peers and administrators at the department and higher levels in the evaluation and shall ensure that a faculty member may attach a concise response to the evaluation;

(2) The proposed procedures for the sustained performance evaluation shall be available to faculty members and to the UFF for review prior to final approval.

(c) Faculty members' Annual Evaluation Summary Form along with attachments, including the documents contained in the evaluation file, shall be the sole basis for the sustained performance evaluation.

(1) A faculty member who received "Meets FSU's High Expectations" or better as an Overall result on her or his Annual Evaluation Summary Form during the previous six years shall not be rated below "Meets FSU's High Expectations" in the sustained performance evaluation, nor subject to a PIP. Faculty whose performance falls below "Meets FSU's High Expectations" in more than two of the previous six evaluations shall develop a performance improvement plan, as specified in 10.5.

10.9   Proficiency in Spoken English. No faculty member shall be evaluated as deficient in oral English language skills unless proved deficient in accordance with the appropriate procedures and examinations for testing such deficiency.

(a) Faculty members involved in classroom instruction, other than in courses conducted primarily in a foreign language or courses not requiring facility in spoken English, who are found by their supervisor, as part of the annual evaluation, to be potentially deficient in English oral language skills, shall be tested in accordance with appropriate procedures and examinations established herein for testing such skills. No reference to an alleged deficiency shall appear in the annual evaluation or in the personnel file of a faculty member who achieves a satisfactory examination score determining proficiency in oral English as specified in the rule (currently "50" or above on the Test of Spoken English).

(b) Faculty members who score at a specified level on an examination established herein for testing oral English language skills ("45" on the Test of Spoken English), may continue to be involved in classroom instruction up to one (1) semester while enrolled in appropriate English language instruction, as described in paragraph (d) below, provided the appropriate administrator determines that the quality of instruction will not suffer. Only such faculty members who demonstrate, on the basis of examinations established by statute and rule, that they are no longer deficient in oral English language skills may be involved in classroom instruction beyond one (1) semester.

(c) Faculty members who score below a minimum score on an examination established herein for determining proficiency in oral English (currently "45" on the Test of Spoken English) shall be assigned appropriate non-classroom duties for the period of oral English language instruction provided by the Board under paragraph (d) below, unless during the period of instruction the faculty member is found, on the basis of an examination specified above, to be no longer deficient in oral English language skills. In that instance, the faculty member will again be eligible for assignment to classroom instructional duties and shall not be disadvantaged by the fact of having been determined to be deficient in oral English language skills.

(d) It is the responsibility of each faculty member who is found, as part of the annual evaluation, to be deficient in oral English language skills by virtue of scoring below the satisfactory score on an examination established herein to take appropriate actions to correct these deficiencies. To assist the faculty member in this endeavor, the Board shall provide appropriate oral English language instruction without cost to such faculty members for a period consistent with their length of appointment and not to exceed two (2) consecutive semesters. The time the faculty member spends in such instruction shall not be considered part of the individual assignment or time worked, nor shall the faculty member be disadvantaged by the fact of participation in such instruction.

(e) If the Board determines, as part of the annual evaluation, that one (1) or more administrations of a test to determine proficiency in oral English language skills is necessary, in accordance with this section, the Board shall pay the expenses for up to two (2) administrations of the test. The faculty member shall pay for additional testing that may be necessary.

10.10   Employee Assistance Programs. Neither the fact of a faculty member's participation in an employee assistance program nor information generated by participation in the program shall be used as evidence of a performance deficiency within the evaluation process described in this Article, except for information relating to a faculty member's failure to participate in an employee assistance program consistent with the terms to which the faculty member and the Board have agreed.

Article 11
EVALUATION FILE

11.1   Policy.
(a) There shall be one (1) evaluation file containing a dated copy of all documents used in the evaluation process including the binder prepared for the purposes of tenure or promotion decisions.

(b) When evaluations and other personnel decisions are made, the only documents that shall be used are those contained in the evaluation file.

(c) The custodian of the evaluation file shall place such documents in the evaluation file and give a copy to the faculty member promptly when it is placed in the evaluation file, unless it is material submitted by the faculty member.

(d) Faculty members shall be notified of the location of the evaluation file and the identity of the custodian. A notice specifying the location of the evaluation file shall be posted in each department/unit.

11.2   Access.
(a) A faculty member may examine the faculty member's evaluation file, upon request, during the regular business hours of the department/unit office in which the file is kept, and under such conditions as are necessary to ensure its integrity and safekeeping.

(b) Upon request, a faculty member may paginate with successive whole numbers the materials in the faculty member's evaluation file.

(c) The faculty member may attach a concise statement in response to any item in the faculty member's evaluation file.

(d) Upon request to the custodian of the evaluation file, a faculty member is entitled to one (1) free copy of any material in the evaluation file. Additional copies may be obtained by the faculty member upon the payment of a reasonable fee for photocopying.

(e) A person designated by the faculty member may examine that faculty member's evaluation file with the written authorization of the faculty member concerned, and subject to the same limitations on access that are applicable to the faculty member.

11.3   Indemnification.
The UFF agrees to indemnify and hold the Board, its officials, agents, and representatives harmless from and against any and all liability for any improper, illegal, or unauthorized use by the UFF of information contained in such evaluation files.

11.4   Use of Evaluative Materials.
In the event a grievance is filed, the Board, the UFF grievance representatives, the arbitrator, and the grievant shall have the right to use, in the grievance proceedings, copies of materials from the grievant's evaluation file.

11.5   Anonymous Material.
There shall be no anonymous materials in the evaluation file except for numerical summaries of student evaluations of teaching that are part of a regular evaluation procedure of classroom instruction and/or written comments from students obtained as part of that regular evaluation

procedure. If written comments from students in a course are included in the evaluation file, all of the comments obtained in the same course must be included.

11.6 Peer Committee Evaluations.

Evaluative materials, or summaries thereof, prepared by peer committees as part of a regular evaluation system, may be placed in an evaluation file when signed by a representative of the committee.

11.7 Removal of Contents.

(a) Materials shown to be contrary to fact shall be removed from the file.

(b) This section shall not authorize the removal of materials from the evaluation file when there is a dispute concerning a matter of judgment or opinion rather than fact.

(c) Materials may also be removed pursuant to the resolution of a grievance.

(d) The custodian may remove duplicative or outdated materials, such as superseded curriculum vitae or student course evaluation materials, if such removal is specifically authorized by the department/unit faculty evaluation criteria and procedures approved pursuant to Article 10.

11.8 Limited Access Information.

(a) Information reflecting evaluation of a faculty member's performance shall be available for inspection only by the faculty member, the faculty member's representative, University officials who use the information in carrying out their responsibilities, peer committees responsible for evaluating faculty performance, and arbitrators or others engaged by the parties to resolve disputes, or by others by court order.

(b) Such limited access status shall not apply to summary data that are required by law to be made available by the University to the public.

Article 12
NON-REAPPOINTMENT

12.1 No Property Right. No appointment shall create any right, interest, or expectancy in any other appointment beyond its specific terms, except as provided in Sections 13.2 and Article 15.

12.2 Notice.

(a) All faculty members, except those described in (b) below are entitled to the following written notice that they will not be offered further appointment:

(1) For faculty members in their first two (2) years of continuous University service, one semester (or its equivalent, 19.5 weeks, for faculty members appointed for more than an academic year);

(2) For faculty members with two (2) or more years of continuous University service, one

year; or

(3) For faculty members with Fixed-term Multi-Year Appointments as defined in Article 8.6, notice shall be given as described in that article, but shall not be less than provided in article 12.2(a)(1-2) above.

(4) For faculty members who are on "soft money", e.g., contracts and grants, sponsored research funds, and grants and donations trust funds, who had five (5) or more years of continuous University service as of June 30, 1991, one year.

(5) The provision of notice under this section does not provide rights to a summer appointment beyond those provided in Article 8.

(b) Faculty members who are on "soft money", e.g., contracts and grants, sponsored research funds, and grants and donations trust funds, except those described in Section 12.2(a)(3), above, are entitled to the following written notice that they will not be offered further appointment:

(1) For faculty members in their first five (5) years of continuous University service, thirty (30) days notice shall be provided contingent upon funds being available in the contract or grant from which the faculty member's salary is funded; or

(2) For faculty members with five (5) or more years of continuous University service, ninety (90) days notice shall be provided contingent upon funds being available in the contract or grant from which the faculty member's salary is funded.

(c) Faculty members who are appointed for less than one (1) academic year, who are appointed to a visiting appointment, and faculty members employed in an auxiliary entity, are not entitled to notice that they will not be offered further appointment, and the statement in (d), below, shall be included in their employment contracts.

(d) Faculty members described (c), above, shall have the following statement included in their employment contracts:

Your employment under this contract will cease on the date indicated. No further notice of cessation of employment is required.

(e) A faculty member who is entitled to written notice of non-reappointment in accordance with the provisions of Section 12.2 who receives written notice that the faculty member will not be offered further appointment shall be entitled, upon written request within twenty (20) days following receipt of such notice, to a written statement of the basis for the decision not to reappoint. Thereafter, the President or representative shall provide such statement within twenty (20) days following receipt of such request. All such notices and statements are to be sent by certified mail, return receipt requested, or delivered in person to the faculty member with written documentation of receipt obtained.

12.3   Grievability. A faculty member who receives written notice of non-reappointment may, according to Article 20, contest the decision because of an alleged violation of a specific term of the Agreement or because of an alleged violation of the faculty member's constitutional rights.

Such grievances must be filed within thirty (30) days of receipt of the statement of the basis for the decision not to reappoint pursuant to Section 12.2(e) or receipt of the notice of non-reappointment if no statement is requested.

12.4   Non-Reappointment Considerations. If the decision not to reappoint was based solely upon adverse financial circumstances, reallocation of resources, reorganization of degree or curriculum offerings or requirements, reorganization of academic or administrative structures, programs, or functions, and/or curtailment or abolition of one or more programs or functions, the University shall take the following actions:

(a) Make a reasonable effort to locate appropriate alternative or equivalent employment first within the University; and

(b) Offer such faculty member, who is not otherwise employed in an equivalent full-time position, re-employment in the same or similar position at the University for a period of two years following the initial notice of non-reappointment, should an opportunity for such re-employment arise. For this purpose, it shall be the faculty member's responsibility to keep the University advised of the faculty member's current address. Any offer of re-employment pursuant to this section must be accepted within fifteen (15) days after the date of the offer, such acceptance to take effect not later than the beginning of the semester immediately following the date the offer was made. In the event such offer of re-employment is not accepted, the faculty member shall receive no further consideration pursuant to this Article.

12.5   Resignation. A faculty member who wishes to resign has the professional obligation, when possible, to provide the University with at least one semester's notice. Upon resignation, all consideration for tenure and reappointment shall cease.

12.6   Notice Document. Notice of appointment and non-reappointment shall not be contained in the same document.

Article 13
LAYOFF AND RECALL

13.1(a) Layoff. When a layoff is to occur as a result of adverse financial circumstances; reallocation of resources; reorganization of degree or curriculum offerings or requirements; reorganization of academic or administrative structures, programs, or functions; or curtailment or abolition of one or more programs or functions; the University shall notify the local UFF Chapter and the UFF state office no less than thirty (30) days prior to taking such action. The UFF may request a consultation with the President or his representatives pursuant to Article 2 during this period to discuss the layoff.

(b) Layoff Unit. The layoff unit may be at an organizational level of the University, such as a campus, division, college/unit, school, department/unit, area, program, or other level of organization as the University deems appropriate.

August 2015

Article 13
LAYOFF AND RECALL

13.2   Layoff Considerations. The selection of faculty members in the layoff unit to be laid off will be determined as follows:

(a) No tenured faculty member shall be laid off if there are un-tenured faculty members in the layoff unit.

(b) No faculty member in a non-tenured position in the layoff unit with more than five (5) years of continuous University service shall be laid off if there are any non-tenured faculty members with five (5) years or less service in the layoff unit.

(c) The sole instance in which only one (1) faculty member will constitute a layoff unit is when the functions that the faculty member performs constitute an area, program, or other level of organization at the University.

(d) The provisions of 13.2(a) and (b) will apply unless the University determines that an Affirmative Action employment program will be adversely affected. When an Affirmative Action Program has been so affected, the University shall notify the UFF in writing.

(e) Where faculty members are equally qualified under (a) or (b) above, those faculty members will be retained who, in the judgment of the University, will best contribute to the mission and purpose of the institution. In making such judgment, the University shall carefully consider faculty members' length of continuous University service, and shall take into account other appropriate factors, including but not limited to performance evaluation by students, peers, and supervisors, and the faculty member's academic training, professional reputation, teaching effectiveness, research record or quality of the creative activity in which the faculty member may be engaged, and service to the profession, community, and public.

(f) No tenured faculty member shall be laid off solely for the purpose of creating a vacancy to be filled by an administrator entering the bargaining unit.

(g) The University shall notify the local UFF Chapter in writing regarding the use of adjunct and other non-unit faculty in those departments/units where faculty members have been laid off. The use of adjunct and other non-unit faculty in departments/units where faculty members have been laid off may be the subject of consultation meetings pursuant to Article 2.

13.3   Alternative/Equivalent Employment. The University shall make a reasonable effort to locate appropriate alternate or equivalent employment for laid-off faculty members within the University and to make known the results of the effort to the person affected.

13.4   Notice. Faculty members should be informed of layoff as soon as practicable and, where circumstances permit, faculty members with three or more years of continuous University service should be provided at least one (1) year's notice; those with less service with at least six (6) month's notice. Faculty members who have received notice of layoff shall be afforded the recall rights granted under Sections 13.3 and 13.5. Formal written notice of layoff is to be sent by certified mail, return receipt requested, or delivered in person to the faculty member with written documentation of receipt obtained. The notice shall include effective date of layoff; reason for layoff; reason for shortened period of notification, if applicable; a statement of recall rights; a statement of appeal/grievance rights and applicable deadlines for filing; and a statement that the faculty member is eligible for consideration for retraining under the provision of Article 22 for a period of two years following layoff.

13.5   Re-employment/Recall.

(a) For a period of two years following layoff, a faculty member who has been laid off and who is not otherwise employed in an equivalent full-time position shall be offered re-employment in the same or similar position at the University at which previously employed at the time of layoff, should an opportunity for such reemployment arise. For this purpose, it shall be the faculty member's responsibility to keep the University advised of the faculty member's current address. Any offer of re-employment pursuant to this section must be accepted within fifteen (15) days after the date of the offer, such acceptance to take effect not later than the beginning of the semester immediately following the date the offer was made. In the event such offer of re-employment is not accepted, the faculty member shall receive no further consideration pursuant to this Article. The University shall notify the local UFF Chapter when an offer of re-employment is issued.

(b) A faculty member who held a tenured appointment on the date of termination by reason of layoff shall resume the tenured appointment upon recall.

(c) The faculty member shall receive the same credit for years of service for purposes of layoff as held on the date of layoff.

(d) Employee Assistance Programs. Consistent with the University's Employee Assistance Program, faculty members participating in an employee assistance program who receive a notice of layoff may continue to participate in that program for a period of ninety (90) days following the layoff.

13.6   Limitations. The provisions of Sections 13.2 through 13.5 of this Agreement shall not apply to those faculty members described in Sections 12.2(a)(3), (b), and (c).

Article 14
PROMOTION

14.1   Policy. Promotion decisions are not merely a totaling of a faculty member's performance evaluations. Rather, the University, through faculty and administrative review, assesses the faculty member's potential for growth and scholarly contribution, as evidenced by the faculty member's record, as well as past meritorious performance. Promotion in the tenured and tenure-earning ranks is attained through meritorious performance in teaching, research or other scholarly activities, and service. Promotion in other faculty classifications is attained through meritorious performance of duties in the faculty member's present position. Administrators who are in the tenured and tenure-earning ranks and are being considered for promotion must qualify on the basis of the criteria as stated in this article rather than on the basis of their administrative duties.

14.2   Criteria and Procedures for Promotion.
    (a) Promotion decisions shall be a result of meritorious performance and shall be based upon established criteria and procedures specified in writing by the University. Such criteria and procedures shall be consistent with the provisions of this Agreement.

    (b) The University criteria and procedures for promotion shall be refined and adapted by each department/unit to reflect, as appropriate, the particular practices of the department's disciplines. Such refinements or adaptations shall be developed and approved by the faculty of the unit to which they apply, in a manner consistent with applicable bylaws of the unit, and shall be consistent with the University criteria and procedures and the provisions of this Agreement.

    (c) Promotion criteria and procedures shall be available in the department/unit office and/or at the college/unit level, and posted on the websites of the corresponding organizational units if they have websites.

    (d) Basis for Promotion Decision. The promotion decision shall take into account the following:
        (1) Second and Fourth Year Reports for Assistant Professors and Progress Toward Promotion letters for all other faculty members;
        (2) Annual assignments;
        (3) Fulfillment of the department/unit written promotion criteria, as related to the candidate's assignments;
        (4) Whether, pursuant to Article 9 Assignment of Responsibilities, the candidate has been provided equal opportunities, in relation to other faculty in the same department, meet the promotion criteria; and
        (5) Evidence of effective performance of assigned responsibilities. Examples of such evidence for teaching include syllabi and peer evaluations of teaching. The evaluation of teaching may not be based primarily on student perceptions.

    (e) Progress toward promotion.
        (1) Faculty members eligible for promotion shall be apprised annually in writing of their progress toward promotion. The appraisal shall be included in the annual evaluation.
        (2) The faculty member may request, in writing, a meeting with an administrator at the next higher level to discuss concerns regarding the promotion appraisal that were not resolved in previous discussions with the evaluator.

14.3   Modification of University Criteria and Procedures for Promotion.

(a) No criteria or procedures for promotion shall be applied to a member of the bargaining unit if they are inconsistent with a provision of this Agreement.

(b) No change in promotion criteria or procedures that would be inconsistent with a provision of this Agreement shall be made without entering into collective bargaining negotiations with the UFF, unless the UFF Chapter agrees to the changes in writing.

(c) The University may modify the criteria or procedures for promotion, so long as the modifications are consistent with the provisions of this Agreement and the UFF Chapter has been notified of the proposed modifications and offered an opportunity to discuss them in consultation with the University President or representative.

(d) Any proposal to develop or modify criteria or procedures for promotion shall be available for discussion by members of the affected departments/units before adoption.

(e) The UFF Chapter must be provided with a copy of any proposed changes in the criteria or procedures for promotions.

(f) Changes in criteria or procedures shall not become effective until one (1) year following adoption of the changes, unless an earlier adoption date is mutually agreed to in writing by the UFF Chapter President and the University President or representative. The date of adoption shall be the date on which the changes are approved in writing by the Board or its representative and, where required, the UFF.

14.4   Recommendations.
(a) Recommendations for promotion shall begin with the faculty member's supervisor and shall be submitted to the appropriate officials for review.

(b) Prior to the consideration of the faculty member's promotion, the faculty member shall have the right to review the contents of the promotion binder and may attach a brief response to any material therein. It shall be the responsibility of the faculty member to see that the binder is complete at that time. The provisions of Sections 11.2 through 11.8 of this Agreement shall apply to the contents of the promotion binder.

(c) Recommendations for promotion shall include a copy of applicable promotion criteria, a narrative explanation provided by each committee in the promotion process summarizing the meeting, the faculty member's annual assignments and the faculty member's promotion reports as outlined in Article 14.2(d)(1).

(d) If any material is added to the file after the commencement of consideration, a copy shall be sent to the faculty member within five (5) business days (by personal delivery or by mail, return receipt requested). The faculty member may attach a brief response within five (5) business days of his/her receipt of the added material. The file shall not be forwarded until either the faculty member submits a response or until five (5) business days after the faculty member received a copy of the added material, whichever occurs first.

(e) The only documents that may be considered in making a promotion recommendation are those contained or referenced in the promotion file.

(f) There shall be only one file if a faculty member is being recommended for both promotion and tenure.

(g) Any contents of the promotion file that are not copies of material already in the one evaluation file specified in Article 11 shall become part of the faculty member's one evaluation file.

(h) The promotion binder shall be reviewed by a faculty committee, which shall make a recommendation on the promotion by secret ballot.

(1) Each department/unit shall have one such committee, elected by the faculty according to the process defined in the bylaws of the department/unit, which is charged with the responsibility of reviewing the records of all prospective candidates for promotion in that department/unit and recommending action on the nomination of each candidate. If a department/unit has fewer than 10 faculty members, and the bylaws of the department/unit do not provide for a faculty committee for review of promotions, the faculty of the department/unit shall be combined with similarly situated department/units determined by the President or designee to elect a joint faculty committee.

(2) For those department/units with tenure-track faculty members, this committee will be the promotion and tenure committee specified in Appendix I 1.3(b), and shall include a majority of tenured faculty members.

(3) Consistent with Article 32 Definitions and usage throughout this CBA, the term "department/unit" as used in this section applies to the college/unit for those college/units that are not organized internally into department/units.

14.5 Promotion Decision.

(a) The President shall make the promotion decision after receiving the advice of the various Promotion and Tenure Committees. The President shall notify the faculty member in writing of the decision.

(b) If any faculty member is denied promotion, he or she shall be notified in writing by the appropriate administrative official, as soon as possible, of that decision. Upon written request by a faculty member within twenty (20) days of the faculty member's receipt of such decision, the University shall provide the faculty member with a written statement of the reasons that the promotion was denied.

14.6 Further Details. Appendices I and J specify further details regarding the criteria and procedures for granting promotion, and tenure where applicable, for specific categories of faculty members.

Article 15
TENURE

15.1 Definition and Policy.

(a) Tenure is one of the principal means by which the quality of the University is maintained and developed and is an indispensable element of any university of quality. Institutions of higher education are conducted for the common good. The common good depends upon the unfettered search for truth and its free exposition. Academic freedom and tenure exist in order that society may have the benefit of honest judgment and independent criticism. Tenure is a condition attained by a faculty member through exemplary teaching, research and other creative or scholarly activities, service, and contributions to the University and to society.

(b) A faculty member who has been granted tenure shall have the status of a permanent member of the faculty and remain in the employment of the University, guaranteed annual reappointment for the academic year, until the faculty member:

(1) voluntarily resigns,

(2) voluntarily retires,

(3) is terminated for just cause in accordance with the provisions of Article 16 Disciplinary Action and Job Abandonment of this Agreement, or

(4) is laid off pursuant to the provisions of Article 13 Layoff and Recall of this Agreement.

(c) Tenure decisions shall be based on the faculty member's performance of assigned duties and responsibilities. Those assignments should be made with full knowledge of the applicable promotion and tenure criteria.

15.2 Eligibility.

(a) Faculty members with the rank of Associate Professor and Professor shall be eligible for tenure.

(b) Non-tenured faculty members in the ranks of Assistant Professor, Associate Professor, and Professor shall be tenure-earning. The Board may designate other positions as tenure-earning and shall notify the faculty member of such status at the time of initial appointment.

(c) Tenure shall be in an academic department/unit.

(d) Tenure shall not extend to administrative appointments.

(e) Credited Tenure-Earning Service.

(1) For a faculty member appointed to a tenure-earning position, the number of years of

credit for prior tenure-earning service that will count toward the faculty member's eligibility for tenure shall be agreed upon in writing at the time of employment.

(2) The number of years of credit for prior service may not be more than two years for a faculty member hired as an assistant professor, not more than three years for a faculty member hired as an associate professor, and not more than four years for a faculty member hired as a professor.

(3) Where a faculty member is credited with tenure-earning service at the time of initial appointment, all or a portion of such credit may be withdrawn, one time, by the faculty member prior to such time that the faculty member becomes eligible to be considered by the departmental promotion and tenure committee.

(f) Tenure-earning Service.

(1) One year of tenure-earning service shall mean employment during at least thirty-nine (39) weeks of any twelve-month period, beginning with the Fall term. Employment for one semester (or its equivalent) shall count as one-half year of tenure-earning service.

(2) Part-time service of a faculty member employed at least one semester in any twelve (12) month period shall be accumulated. For example, two (2) semesters of half-time service shall be considered one-half year of service toward the period of tenure-earning service.

(3) Contingent upon a written agreement between the faculty member and the Board, time spent by a faculty member under joint appointment or exchange on a duly established personnel exchange program of the University, or on a special assignment for the benefit of the University, shall be counted toward the fulfillment of eligibility for tenure.

(4) Extension of Tenure-Earning Period for Personal Circumstances. Personal circumstances are individual or family situations that substantially impede progress toward tenure, whether or not such circumstances require or justify a leave of absence under the provisions of this Agreement or University rules. A faculty member may request an extension of one year from the chair with the approval of the president and dean or representative due to qualifying personal circumstances, before being considered for tenure.

a. Personal circumstances shall be defined as including, but not limited to: childbirth or adoption; personal injury or illness; care of ill or injured dependents; elder care; death of a closely related family member resulting in need for extended dependent care.

b. The Board shall notify the faculty member in writing of the decision on the request for the extension of time due to qualifying personal circumstances. Such notification shall be issued no later than sixty (60) days from the time the faculty member requests the extension.

c. In order to receive an extension of the period for earning tenure under this Section, the advent of the qualifying personal circumstance impeding progress toward tenure must be prior to the May 15 preceding the academic year in which the faculty member is scheduled to be formally considered for tenure.

d. Whether a faculty member has requested or received an extension of the tenure earning period shall not be considered in deciding whether to award tenure.

e. This policy is separate from and independent of the provisions in Article 17 for extending the period for earning tenure.

f. The decision of the chair, dean, and president or representative shall be final and not subject to the grievance procedure of this agreement.

(5) During the period of tenure-earning service, continuation of the faculty member's employment shall be governed by the provisions of Article 12.

15.3   Criteria and Procedures for Tenure.

(a) The decision to award tenure to a faculty member shall be a result of meritorious performance and shall be based on established criteria specified in writing by the University. Such criteria and procedures shall be consistent with the provisions of this agreement.

(b) The University criteria and procedures for tenure shall be refined and adapted by each department/unit to reflect, as appropriate, the particular practices of the department's disciplines. Such refinements or adaptations shall be developed and approved by the faculty of the unit to which they apply, in a manner consistent with applicable bylaws of the unit, and shall be consistent with the University criteria and procedures and the provisions of this agreement.

(c) Tenure criteria and procedures shall be available in the department/unit office and/or at the college/unit level, and posted on the websites of the corresponding organizational units if they have websites.

(d) Basis for Tenure Decision. The decision shall take into account the following:
(1) Second and Fourth Year Reports for Assistant Professors and "Progress Toward Tenure" letters for all other faculty member;
(2) annual assignments;
(3) the needs of the department/unit, college/unit, and University;
(4) the contributions of the faculty member to his/her academic unit (program, department/unit, college/unit); and
(5) the contributions the faculty member is expected to make to the institution in the future; and
(6) evidence of effective performance in all the areas of responsibility normally assigned to a tenured faculty member. Examples of such evidence for teaching include syllabi and peer evaluations of teaching. The evaluation of teaching may not be based primarily on student perceptions.

(e) Progress toward tenure.
(1) The University shall give a copy of the criteria and procedures for tenure to tenure-earning faculty members.
(2) Tenure-earning faculty members shall be apprised in writing once each year of their progress toward tenure. The appraisal shall be included in the annual evaluation.
(3) Assistant Professors shall receive a tenure review in their second and fourth years. These reviews are mentoring opportunities during which the department/unit's Promotion and

Tenure Committee shall provide specific feedback and advice reflecting expectations for tenure and how the faculty member is progressing toward meeting those expectations. The faculty member shall meet with the department/unit's chair to discuss the report. Both the "Second Year Report" and the "Fourth Year Report" shall be included in the tenure binder. Assistant Professors hired with credit toward tenure shall have credited years included in the determination of the timing of second and fourth year reviews unless an alternative schedule is mutually agreed upon by the faculty member and his or her supervisor.

(4) The faculty member may request, in writing, a meeting with an administrator at the next higher level to discuss any concerns regarding tenure appraisals that were not resolved in previous discussions with the evaluator.

15.4   Modification of Criteria and Procedures.

(a) No criteria or procedures for tenure shall be applied to a member of the bargaining unit if they are inconsistent with a provision of this Agreement.

(b) No change in tenure criteria or procedures that would be inconsistent with a provision of this Agreement shall be made without entering into collective bargaining negotiations with the UFF, unless the UFF Chapter agrees to the changes in writing.

(c) The University may modify the criteria or procedures for tenure, so long as the modifications are consistent with the provisions of this Agreement and the UFF Chapter has been notified of the proposed modifications and offered an opportunity to discuss them in consultation with the University President or representative.

(d) Any proposal to develop or modify criteria or procedures for tenure shall be available for discussion by members of the affected departments/units before adoption.

(e) The UFF Chapter must be provided with a copy of any proposed change in the criteria or procedures for tenure.

(f) Changes in criteria or procedures shall not become effective until one (1) year following adoption of the changes, unless an earlier effective date is mutually agreed to in writing by the UFF Chapter President and the University President or representative. The date of adoption shall be the date on which the changes are approved in writing by the Board or its representative and the UFF has been notified.

(g) Effect on Faculty. The provisions of Article 9 are applicable to the modified criteria. Further, if a faculty member has at least three (3) years of tenure-earning credit as of the date on which changes in the tenure criteria are adopted pursuant to this Article, the faculty member shall be evaluated for tenure under the criteria as they existed prior to modification unless the faculty member notifies the University at least thirty (30) days prior to commencement of the tenure consideration that he/she chooses to be evaluated under the newly-adopted criteria.

15.5   Recommendations.

(a) Recommendations for tenure shall begin with the faculty member's supervisor and shall include a poll by secret ballot and a narrative explanation summarizing the meeting of the tenured members of the faculty member's department/unit and elected promotion and tenure committee. If there are fewer than three tenured faculty members in the candidate faculty member's department/unit, the University president or his/her designee shall appoint additional tenured faculty members from related departments/units to form a tenure evaluation committee of at least three tenured faculty members to be polled by secret ballot. The performance of a faculty member during the entire term of tenure-earning employment at the institution shall be considered in determining whether to grant tenure. Prior to the consideration of candidacy, the faculty member shall have the right to review the contents of the tenure file and may attach a brief and concise response to any materials therein; it shall be the responsibility of the faculty member to see that the file is complete at that time. The provisions of Article 11 of this Agreement shall apply to the contents of the tenure file.

(b) Recommendations regarding tenure shall include a copy of applicable tenure criteria, the faculty member's annual assignments, Second and Fourth Year Reports for Assistant Professors, the narrative explanation provided by each committee in the process summarizing the meetings, and "Progress Toward Tenure" letters.

(c) If any material is added to the file after the commencement of consideration, a copy shall be sent to the faculty member within five (5) business days (by personal delivery or by mail, return receipt requested). The faculty member may attach a brief response within five (5) business days of his/her receipt of the added material. The file shall not be forwarded until either the faculty member submits a response or until five (5) business days after the faculty member received a copy of the added material, whichever occurs first.

(d) The only documents that may be considered in making a tenure recommendation are those contained or referenced in the tenure file.

(e) There shall be only one file if a faculty member is being recommended for both promotion and tenure.

(f) Any contents of the promotion file that are not copies of material already in the one evaluation file specified in Article 11 shall become part of the faculty member's one evaluation file.

15.6 Tenure Decision.

(a) Time of Consideration.

(1) A faculty member shall normally be considered for tenure during the sixth year of continuous service in a tenure-earning position including any prior service credit granted at the time of initial employment.

(2) With the approval of his or her dean, a faculty member may be considered for tenure

during his or her fifth year of continuous service. The criteria for tenure shall be identical to the criteria applied to faculty members who are considered in their sixth year.

(b) Nature of Decision. By the end of six (6) years of tenure-earning service at the University, including time credited as tenure-earning service at the time of appointment, a faculty member eligible for tenure shall either be awarded tenure by the President and reported to the Board or given notice that further employment will not be offered pursuant to Article 12.

(c) Withdrawal from Consideration. A faculty member being considered for tenure prior to the sixth (6) year may withdraw from consideration at any level without prejudice within five (5) working days of being informed of the results of the secret ballot vote.

(d) Action by the Board. The Board shall confirm the President's award of tenure, based on the results of the faculty peer-review process. This action shall normally be taken at the Spring Board Meeting. The President shall notify the faculty member of the Board's action in writing immediately, or as soon thereafter as possible but in no case later than five (5) days after the meeting at which the action is taken.

(e) Notice of Denial. Upon written request by a faculty member within twenty (20) days of the faculty member's receipt of such notice, the University shall provide the faculty member with a written statement of reasons by the President or representative why tenure was not granted.

15.7   Transfer of Tenure. When a tenured faculty member is transferred to another department/unit within the University, the faculty member's tenure shall be transferred to the new department/unit. Such transfer shall be subject to the approval of the tenured faculty in the new department/unit.

15.8   Tenure upon Appointment. Tenure may be granted to a faculty member by the President at the time of initial appointment, subject to review and recommendation by the department/unit and a subcommittee of the University Promotion and Tenure Committee, with final approval by the President.

Article 16
DISCIPLINARY ACTION AND JOB ABANDONMENT

16.1   Just Cause.
(a) The purpose of this article is to provide a prompt and equitable procedure for disciplinary action, which shall be taken only for just cause. Just cause shall be defined as:
    (1) incompetence, or
    (2) misconduct.

(b) A faculty member's activities which fall outside the scope of employment shall constitute misconduct only if such activities adversely affect the legitimate interests of the University.

(c) No provision of this agreement prevents the University from taking disciplinary action for just cause.

16.2   Progressive Discipline. Both parties endorse the principle of progressive discipline as applied to professionals. Progressive discipline is based on the idea that as offenses occur appropriate discipline will be administered in a progressive manner. Penalties shall be appropriate to the circumstances and proportionate to the seriousness of the offense. In prescribing disciplinary actions, it is recognized that some offenses are so serious that suspension or dismissal may be warranted on the first occurrence even though the faculty member has no prior record of having been disciplined. All offenses can have a cumulative effect, and offenses need not be identical to impose a penalty more severe than prescribed for a similar offense. However, the period of reckoning for considering a previous letter of reprimand in determining the level of discipline shall be limited to two years.

(a) The progressive sanctions for disciplinary action that may be imposed on a faculty member include the following:

(1) Written reprimand – a formal written expression of institutional rebuke, which shall contain a description of the misconduct and identify itself as a reprimand.

a.   Written reprimand is distinguished from an informal written or spoken warning, which are not disciplinary actions.

b.   A written reprimand shall be delivered to the recipient and maintained in the faculty member's designated evaluation file.

(2) Suspension with pay for a period of time specified in writing.

a.   The written statement of suspension shall include the precise terms of the suspension. Those terms may include, for example, some or all of the following: loss of normal faculty privileges such as access to University property, participation in departmental government, voting rights, administration of grants, supervision of graduate students, loss of parking or library privileges, and use of University administrative staff.

b.   Suspension as a disciplinary action is to be distinguished from involuntary leave, which is a precautionary action.

c.   A faculty member suspended with pay shall not be expected to perform any functions that depend on privileges that have been suspended

(3) Suspension without pay for a period of time specified in writing, with the same conditions outlined in subsection 16.2(a)(2), above. A faculty member suspended without pay shall not be expected to perform any functions for the University

(4) Demotion to the next lower rank with a reduction in salary not to exceed the percentage for promotion from that rank. The faculty member may apply for promotion to the former rank after a period of two years. A demoted faculty member with tenure shall not be demoted to a lower rank without tenure.

(5) Termination. A faculty member shall be given written notice of termination at least six (6) months in advance of the effective date of such termination, except that in cases where the President or representative determines that a faculty member's actions adversely affect the functioning of the University or jeopardize the safety or welfare of the faculty member,

colleagues, or students, the President or representative may give less than six (6) months notice.

(b) Spoken or written warnings, counseling, or recommendations for participation in an Employee Assistance Program shall not be considered disciplinary action and may not be considered as a substitute for written reprimand in progressive discipline.

16.3 Investigation.

(a) Before questioning a faculty member the University shall inform the faculty member that the investigation may lead to disciplinary action.

(b) A faculty member has a right to request union representation during questioning that may reasonably be expected to result in disciplinary action. This provision shall not obligate the UFF to provide representation for faculty members who are not members of the UFF.

16.4 Notice of Intent to Suspend, Demote, or Terminate. When the President or representative has reason to believe that a suspension, demotion, or termination may be imposed, the President or representative shall provide the faculty member and the UFF with a written notice of the proposed action and the reasons therefore, as well as the faculty member's rights to review specified in Section 16.5 below, if applicable.

(a) Such notice shall be sent via certified mail, return receipt requested, or delivered in person with written documentation of receipt obtained.

(b) The faculty member shall be given twenty (20) days in which to respond in writing to the President or representative before the proposed action is taken. The faculty member may include in his or her response supporting materials from other individuals. The President or representative then may issue a notice of disciplinary action under Section 16.6.

(c) If the President or representative does not issue a notice of disciplinary action within 180 days of Notice of Intent, no disciplinary action shall be taken. If new information pertinent to the initial reason for the investigation becomes available, a new Notice of Intent may be issued.

(d) If the President or representative does not issue a notice of disciplinary action, the notice of proposed disciplinary action shall not be retained in the faculty member's evaluation file.

16.5 Peer Panel. In cases in which the Board has under consideration disciplinary action to suspend, demote, or terminate the appointment of a tenured faculty member, or to terminate the appointment of an untenured tenure-track faculty member prior to the expiration of the faculty member's current employment contract, the faculty member shall be provided with the opportunity for a review by an appropriate faculty committee as described in paragraph (e) below (hereinafter referred to as the "Peer Panel" or the "Panel") prior to issuance of the Notice of Discipline. This peer panel shall serve as the peer review panel specified in Regulation 6C2-1.004(6)(b)3, Florida Administrative Code (Article VI, Section B, paragraph 3.a of the University Constitution).

(a) The process provided hereby consists of the opportunity to submit written materials to the Peer Panel, whose members shall individually and independently consider the evidence and submit separate recommendations reflecting their individual points of view to the President or representative.

(b) This process shall not waive the right of a faculty member to file a grievance in accordance with this CBA, or any other adjudicatory due process proceeding following the issuance of a final Notice of Discipline.

(c) Alternatives. As an alternative to the peer review panel, the faculty member may elect to meet with the President or representative, in addition to submitting a written statement to the President or representative as provided by Section 16.4. Such election must be made in writing and delivered to the office of the President or representative within ten (10) calendar days of receipt of the notice of intent to suspend, demote, or terminate.

(d) The faculty member's failure to timely request the peer panel or, in the alternative, to follow through with a timely meeting with the President or representative, will constitute a waiver by the faculty member of further proceedings under Section 16.5. Failure of the faculty member to submit a timely written statement to the Peer Panel will constitute a waiver of the opportunity to submit a written statement. In that event, the Panel will offer its opinions based on the written material submitted by the President or representative.

(e) Peer Panel. Upon the timely request for a peer panel, the President or representative will immediately inform the Chairperson of the Faculty Senate Grievance Committee (hereinafter referred to as the "Chairperson"), who will within ten (10) calendar days of being informed establish, from among the members of that Committee, three (3) faculty members who will participate individually and independently as the Peer Panel. The Chairperson will notify the President or representative, the UFF Grievance Chair, and the faculty member of the establishment of the Peer Panel.

(f) Submission of Information. Upon establishment of the Panel, the President or representative will submit to the Chairperson written materials to be considered by the Panel, including the notice of the proposed action and the reasons therefore, with a copy to the faculty member and the UFF Grievance Chair. Within ten (10) calendar days thereafter, the faculty member may provide to the Chairperson, with a copy to the President or representative and the UFF Grievance Chair, a written statement or response to the President or representative's notice and reasons, and any additional written documentation to be considered by the Panel. The Chairperson will transmit copies of the foregoing information and/or documentation to the Panel immediately upon receipt thereof. The Peer Panel may seek additional information from either party as it deems necessary. The UFF Grievance Chair shall be provided with copies of any such additional information.

(g) Recommendations. The members of the Panel will individually evaluate and consider the notice of the proposed action and the reasons therefore and any additional documentation submitted by the President or representative and the faculty member and, within ten (10) calendar days of the deadline for submissions specified in (f) above, will submit to the President or representative individual written and signed recommendations, with copies thereof to the faculty member and the UFF Grievance Chair. The recommendation shall, express the Panel members' individual opinions as to whether disciplinary action is warranted for the alleged offense and, if so, the penalty deemed appropriate under the circumstances.

(h) Consideration of Recommendations. The President or representative will review the Panel recommendations and take them into consideration in deciding whether the University should initiate discipline and issue the Notice of Discipline pursuant to Section 16.6. Pursuant to Section 16.2, if the President or representative does not issue a notice of disciplinary action, the notice of proposed disciplinary action shall not be retained in the faculty member's evaluation file.

(i) Status of Records. By invoking in writing the Peer Panel process, the faculty member will have consented to the disclosure to the Panel, for purposes of its process, evaluative information. Records maintained for the purposes of any such investigation of misconduct, including but not limited to a complaint against a faculty member and all information obtained pursuant to the investigation of such complaint, shall be confidential until the investigation ceases to be active or until the University provides written notice to the faculty member that the University has either concluded the investigation with a finding not to proceed with disciplinary action; concluded the investigation with a finding to proceed with disciplinary action; or issued a Notice of Intent Letter.

16.6   Final Notice of Discipline. All notices of disciplinary action shall include a statement of the reasons therefore and a statement advising the faculty member that the action is subject to Article 20, Grievance Procedure. All such notices shall be sent via certified mail, return receipt requested, or delivered in person to the faculty member with written documentation of receipt obtained.

16.7   Job Abandonment.
(a) If a faculty member is absent without authorized leave for twelve (12) or more consecutive days under the provisions of Section 17.2, the faculty member shall be considered to have abandoned the position and voluntarily resigned from the University.

(b) Notwithstanding paragraph (a), above, if the faculty member's absence is for reasons beyond the control of the faculty member and the faculty member notifies the University as soon as practicable, the faculty member will not be considered to have abandoned the position.

16.8   Employee Assistance Program. Neither the fact of a faculty member's participation in an employee assistance program, nor information generated by participation in the program, shall be used as a reason for discipline under this Article, except for information relating to a faculty member's failure to participate in an employee assistance program consistent with the terms to which the faculty member and the University have agreed.

Article 17
LEAVES

17.1   Policy and Leave Topics

(a) Policy. Leave is provided in a variety of forms to meet needs of both the University and faculty members and to comply with applicable laws.

(b) Leave Topics in this Article
    (1) Requests for Leave / Extension and Return from Leave (17.2)
    (2) Accrual During Leave with Pay (17.3)
    (3) Tenure Credit During Periods of Leave (17.4)
    (4) Holidays (17.5)
    (5) Family and Medical Leave Act (FMLA) Entitlements (17.6)
    (6) Parental Leave, Paid and Unpaid (17.7)
    (7) Leaves Due to Illness/Injury including Sick Leave (17.8)
    (8) Annual Leave (Paid Vacation) (17.9)
    (9) Administrative Leaves (17.10)
        a. Jury Duty and Court Appearances (17.10(a))
        b. Leave Pending Investigation (17.10(c))
        c. Other Leaves Not Affecting Leave Balances (17.10(d))
        d. Official Emergency Closings (17.10(e))
        e. Bereavement Leave (17.10(f))
    (10)   Military Leave (17.11)
    (11)   Further Provisions on Leave Without Pay (17.12)

17.2   Requests for Leave or Leave and Return from Leave.

(a) For a leave of one (1) semester or more, a faculty member shall make a written request not less than 120 days prior to the beginning of the proposed leave, if practicable.

(b) For an extension of a leave of one (1) semester or more, a faculty member shall make a written request not less than sixty (60) days before the end of the leave, if practicable.

(c) The University shall approve or deny such request in writing not later than thirty (30) days after receipt of the request.

(d) An absence without approved leave or extension of leave shall subject the faculty member to the provisions of Section 16.7.

(e) A faculty member's request for use of leave for an event covered by the provisions of the Family and Medical Leave Act (FMLA) of 1993 (Public Law 103-3) shall be submitted and responded to in accordance with the provisions of Section 17.6.

(f) A faculty member who returns from an approved leave of absence with or without pay shall be returned to the same classification, unless the University and the faculty member agree in writing to other terms and conditions. The return from FMLA leave shall be in accordance with Section 17.6.

17.3   Accrual During Leave with Pay. A faculty member shall accrue normal leave credits while on compensated leave in full-pay status, or while participating in the sabbatical or professional development programs. If a faculty member is on compensated leave in less than full-pay status for other than sabbaticals or professional development programs, the faculty member shall accrue leave in proportion to the pay status.

17.4   Tenure Credit During Periods of Leave. Semester(s) during which a faculty member is on compensated or uncompensated leave shall not be creditable for the purpose of determining eligibility for tenure, except by mutual agreement of the faculty member and the University. In deciding whether to credit such leave toward tenure eligibility, the President or representative shall consider the duration of the leave, the relevance of the faculty member's activities while on such leave to the faculty member's professional development and to the faculty member's field of employment, the benefits, if any, which accrue to the University by virtue of placing the faculty member on such leave, and other appropriate factors.

17.5   Holidays.
(a) A faculty member shall be entitled to observe all official holidays designated in accordance with Section 110.117, Florida Statutes. No classes shall be scheduled on holidays. Classes not held because of a holiday shall not be rescheduled.

(b) Supervisors are encouraged not to require a faculty member to perform duties on holidays; however, a faculty member required to perform duties on holidays shall have the faculty member's schedule adjusted to provide equivalent time off, up to a maximum of eight (8) hours for each holiday worked.

17.6   Family and Medical Leave Act (FMLA)
(a) The Family and Medical Leave Act of 1993 ("FMLA") is the common name for the federal law providing eligible faculty members an entitlement of up to twelve (12) work weeks (480 hours) of continuous or intermittent leave without pay for qualified family or medical reasons during a one-year period. This Act entitles the faculty member to take leave without pay; where University policies permit, faculty members may use accrued leave with pay during any qualifying family or medical leave. The failure to list, define, or specify any particular provision or portion of the FMLA in this Agreement shall in no way constitute a waiver of any of the rights or benefits conferred to the employer or the faculty member through the FMLA.

(b) FMLA Leave Entitlements.

(1) In the University, a faculty member, whether salaried or paid from Other Personal Services (OPS), is entitled to twelve (12) work weeks of FMLA leave within a rolling twelve (12) month period, measured backward, for any qualifying family or medical leave. FMLA also includes a special leave entitlement that permits eligible employees to take up to 26 weeks of leave to care for a covered service member during a single 12-month period.

(2) If an eligible faculty member elects to take Parental Leave in accordance with the provisions of Section 17.7, up to twelve (12) work weeks of such leave may be counted against that faculty member's FMLA entitlement.

(c) Accounting for the Use of FMLA Leave in a Twelve-Month Period.

(1) A rolling twelve (12) month period is used to count the twelve (12) work weeks referred to in (b) above.

(2) An eligible faculty member's entitlement to leave for a birth or placement for adoption or foster care expires at the end of a twelve (12) month period beginning on the date of the birth or placement of the child.

(d) Use and Approval of FMLA Leave.

(1) The University shall approve FMLA leave for an eligible faculty member as long as the reasons for absence qualify under the FMLA and the faculty member has not exhausted the faculty member's twelve (12) work weeks within the appropriate 12-month period for such leave. The faculty member may request FMLA leave as accrued leave, leave without pay, or a combination of both.

(2) The University may require that the faculty member use accrued leave with pay prior to requesting leave without pay for four hundred and eighty (480) hours (12 workweeks) of FMLA leave. Requiring the use of paid leave shall be applied consistently and may not be used merely to exhaust the faculty member's leave balance in order to prohibit the use of paid leave while on leave without pay as provided for in Section 17.11(e).

(3) After the President or representative has acquired knowledge that the leave is being taken for an FMLA required reason, the President or representative shall within five business days, absent extenuating circumstances, notify the faculty member her/his eligibility and rights and responsibilities under the FMLA.

(e) Medical Certification.

(1) Medical certification is required for all FMLA events; the supervisor will provide the faculty member or the faculty member's spokesperson the Health Care Provider Certification form, to be completed by the attending health care provider.

(2) A fitness for duty statement may be required to affirm the faculty member's ability to return to work and perform one or more of the essential functions of the job within the meaning of the Americans with Disabilities Act (ADA), after being absent on FMLA leave.

August 2015

(f) Return to Position. Upon return from FMLA leave, the faculty member shall be returned to the same or equivalent position in the same class and work location, including the same shift or equivalent schedule, unless the University and the faculty member agree in writing to other conditions and terms under which such leave is to be granted.

(g) Continuation of Benefits. The use of FMLA leave by eligible faculty members shall neither enhance nor decrease any rights or benefits normally accrued to salaried faculty members during a leave with pay or any rights or benefits normally accrued during a leave without pay.

(h) If any provision of Section 17.6 (FMLA) is inconsistent with or in contravention of the Family Medical Leave Act of 1993, Public Law 103-3, or the Family and Medical Leave Act Regulations, 29 CFR Part 825, or any subsequently enacted legislation, then such provision shall be superseded by the laws or regulations referenced above, except to the extent that the collective bargaining agreement or any faculty member benefit program or plan provides greater family or medical leave rights to an eligible faculty member.

17.7   Parental Leaves.

(a) Paid Parental Leave. No more than once in the course of a faculty member's employment at the University, and upon completion of the following conditions, a faculty member shall be granted, upon request, a paid parental leave not to exceed six (6) months, within a year from when the faculty member becomes a biological parent or a child is placed in the faculty member's home for purposes of adoption by the faculty member. Paid parental leave will not be granted to two faculty members for the same birth or adoption. Contract and grant funded faculty members shall be eligible to the extent that such program benefits are permitted by the terms of the contract or grant and the rules of the funding agency, and adequate funds are available for this purpose in the contract or grant.

(1) Commitment to Reimbursement. A faculty member who utilizes this benefit and is eligible for a leave payout upon separation, or upon transfer from an annual leave contract to a non-annual leave accruing contract, shall have the hours utilized in parental leave deducted from his or her gross total accrued leave balance, applying sick leave first. With the exception of section 17.7(a)(2) below, a faculty member whose sick and/or annual leave balance is insufficient to cover the amount of parental leave utilized shall not be responsible for repayment.

(2) Commitment to Return. The faculty member must agree in writing to return to University employment for at least one (1) academic year following participation in the program. A faculty member who fails to fulfill this commitment shall be responsible for repayment of the portion of the parental leave utilized in excess of his or her leave balance. Agreements to the contrary must be reduced to writing.

(3) Notice and Use with Other Leave(s). Paid leave shall not be granted that relieves the faculty member of both teaching and service assignments for more than one semester. This provision does not prohibit deans or chairs from modifying duty assignments before and after the paid leave. The faculty member must request use of the paid parental leave in advance, no later than three (3) months prior to the beginning of the leave. A shorter notice period may be allowed

on a case-by-case basis, for good cause and/or special circumstances, by the faculty member's supervisor. Unless approved in writing by the faculty member's supervisor, paid parental leave may not be used immediately before or after other leave or sabbaticals. Paid parental leave may not be used on a part-time basis unless the faculty member is partially E&G funded; or an agreement has been reduced to writing.

(4) Signed Agreement. The faculty member is required to sign a written agreement detailing the terms of this benefit. Participation in this benefit is contingent upon execution of the signed documentation.

(5) Repayment. Repayment of salary received during parental leave shall be required in those instances where salary is paid in the absence of a signed agreement by the faculty member, or when the faculty member fails to comply with the terms of a signed agreement.

(b) Other Parental Leave.

(1) A faculty member shall be granted a parental leave not to exceed six (6) months when the faculty member becomes a biological parent or a child is placed in the faculty member's home pending adoption; foster care is not covered under parental leave but is provided through the FMLA provisions in accordance with Section 17.6.

(2) If a faculty member plans to use a combination of accrued leave and leave without pay, such request shall include the specific periods for each type of leave requested. Use of accrued leave during an approved period of leave without pay shall be in accordance with Section 17.11(e).

(3) The period of parental leave shall begin no more than two (2) weeks before the expected date of the child's arrival.

a. The President or representative shall acknowledge to the faculty member in writing the period of leave to be granted, that such leave counts against the faculty member's unused FMLA entitlements in accordance with Section 17.6 of this Agreement, and the date of return to employment.

b. At the end of the approved parental leave and at the faculty member's request, the President or representative shall grant part-time leave without pay for a period not to exceed one (1) year, unless the President or representative determines that granting such leave would be inconsistent with the best interests of the University.

c. Any illness caused or contributed to by pregnancy shall be treated as a temporary disability and the faculty member shall be allowed to use accrued sick leave credits when such temporary disability is certified by a health care provider.

d. Upon agreement between the faculty member and the University, intermittent FMLA leave or a reduced work schedule may be approved for the birth of the faculty member's child or placement of a child with the faculty member for adoption in accordance with Section 17.6.

17.8   Leaves Due to Illness/Injury.

Illness/Injury is defined as any physical or mental impairment of health, including such an impairment proximately resulting from pregnancy, which does not allow a faculty member to fully and properly perform the duties of the faculty member's position. When a faculty member's illness/injury may be covered by the Americans with Disabilities Act Amendments Act (ADAAA), the provisions of Public Law 110-335 shall apply.

(a) Sick Leave.

(1) Accrual of Sick Leave.

a. A full-time faculty member shall accrue four (4) hours of sick leave for each biweekly pay period, or the number of hours that are directly proportionate to the number of days worked during less than a full-pay period, without limitation as to the total number of hours that may be accrued.

b. A part-time faculty member shall accrue sick leave at a rate directly proportionate to the percent of time employed.

c. A faculty member appointed under Other Personal Services (OPS) shall not accrue sick leave.

(2) Uses of Sick Leave.

a. Sick leave shall be accrued before being taken, provided that a faculty member who participates in a sick leave pool shall not be prohibited from using sick leave otherwise available to the faculty member through the sick leave pool.

b. Sick leave shall be authorized for the following:

i. The faculty member's personal illness or exposure to a contagious disease which would endanger others.

ii. The faculty member's personal appointments with a health care provider.

iii. The illness or injury of a member of the faculty member's immediate family, at the discretion of the supervisor. Approval of requests for use of reasonable amounts of sick leave for caring for a member of the faculty member's immediate family shall not be unreasonably withheld. "Immediate family" means the spouse, grandparents, parents, brothers, sisters, children, and grandchildren of both the faculty member and the faculty member's spouse, and dependents living in the household.

iv. The death of a member of the faculty member's immediate family, at the discretion of the supervisor. Approval of requests for use of reasonable amounts of sick leave for the death of a member of the faculty member's immediate family shall not be unreasonably withheld.

c. A continuous period of sick leave commences with the first day of absence and includes all subsequent days until the faculty member returns to work. For this purpose, Saturdays, Sundays, and official holidays observed by the state shall not be counted unless the faculty member is scheduled to perform services on such days. During any seven (7) day period, the maximum number of days of sick leave charged against any faculty member shall be five (5).

d. A faculty member who requires the use of sick leave should notify the supervisor as soon as practicable.

e. A faculty member who becomes eligible for the use of sick leave while on approved annual leave shall, upon notifying the supervisor, substitute the use of accrued sick leave to cover such circumstances.

(3) Certification. If a faculty member's request for absence or absence exceeds four (4) consecutive days, or if a pattern of absence is documented, the University may require a faculty member to furnish certification issued by an attending health care provider of the medical reasons necessitating the absence and/or the faculty member's ability to return to work. If the medical certification furnished by the faculty member is not acceptable, the faculty member may be required to submit to a medical examination by a health care provider who is not a University staff member which shall be paid for by the University. If the medical certification indicates that the faculty member is unable to perform assigned duties, the President or representative may place the faculty member on compulsory leave under the conditions set forth in Section 17.8(c).

(4) Transfer of Credits.

a. Upon re-employment with the University within 100 days, the full balance of accrued sick leave shall accompany the faculty member unless the faculty member has received a lump sum payment for accrued sick leave. If a faculty member has received such a lump sum payment, the faculty member may elect in writing, upon re-employment, to restore the faculty member's accrued sick leave. Such restoration will be effective upon repayment of the full lump sum leave payment.

b. When a faculty member moves from a position in a Florida governmental entity (state agency, university, community college, county or city) to a leave-accruing position within the University, the faculty member may transfer up to two hundred and forty (240) hours, or more with the approval of the hiring department, of unused sick leave accrued in the classification and pay plan in which the faculty member was previously employed and for which payment has not been received; however, no more than thirty-one (31) days may elapse between jobs.

c. When a faculty member moves to a position within a governmental entity within Florida the transfer of unused sick leave shall be governed by the rules of the plan to which the faculty member is transferring.

(5) Payment for Unused Sick Leave.

a. A faculty member with fewer than ten (10) years of state service who separates from state government shall not be paid for any unused sick leave.

b. Faculty members hired after May 6, 2011, shall not be paid for any unused sick leave.

c. A faculty member who was hired by the University on or prior to May 6, 2011 and who has completed ten (10) or more years of state service, has not been found guilty or has not admitted to being guilty of committing, aiding, or abetting any embezzlement, theft, or bribery in connection with state government, or has not been found guilty by a court of competent jurisdiction of having violated any state law against or prohibiting strikes by public faculty members, and separates from state government because of retirement for other than disability reasons, termination, or death, shall be compensated at the faculty member's current regular hourly rate of pay for one-eighth of all unused sick leave accrued prior to October 1, 1973, plus one-fourth of all unused sick leave accrued on or after October 1, 1973; provided that one-fourth of the unused sick leave since 1973 does not exceed 480 hours.

d.   Upon layoff, a faculty member with ten (10) or more years of state service shall be paid for unused sick leave as described in paragraph c., above, unless the faculty member requests in writing that unused sick leave be retained pending re-employment. For a faculty member who is re-employed by the University within twelve (12) calendar months following layoff, all unused sick leave shall be restored to the faculty member, provided the faculty member requests such action in writing and repays the full amount of any lump sum leave payments received at the time of layoff. A faculty member who is not re-employed within twelve (12) calendar months following layoff shall be paid for sick leave in accordance with Section 110.122, Florida Statutes.

e.   All payments for unused sick leave authorized by Section 110.122, Florida Statutes, shall be made in lump sum and shall not be used in determining the average final compensation of a faculty member in any state administered retirement system. A faculty member shall not be carried on the payroll beyond the last official day of employment, except that a faculty member who is unable to perform duties because of a disability may be continued on the payroll until all sick leave is exhausted.

f.   In the event of the death of a faculty member who is eligible for a sick leave payout, payment for unused sick leave at the time of death shall be made to the faculty member's beneficiary, estate, or as provided by law.

(b) Job-Related Illness/Injury.

(1) A faculty member who sustains a job-related illness/injury that is compensable under the Workers' Compensation Law shall be carried in full-pay status for a period of medically certified illness/injury not to exceed seven (7) days immediately following the illness/injury, or for a maximum of forty (40) work hours if taken intermittently without being required to use accrued sick or annual leave.

(2) If, as a result of the job-related illness/injury, the faculty member is unable to resume work at the end of the period provided in paragraph (1), above:

a.   The faculty member may elect to use accrued leave in an amount necessary to receive salary payment that will increase the Workers' Compensation payments to the total salary being received prior to the occurrence of the illness/injury. In no case shall the faculty member's salary and Workers' Compensation benefits exceed the amount of the faculty member's regular salary payments; or

b.   The faculty member shall be placed on leave without pay and shall receive normal Workers' Compensation benefits if the faculty member has exhausted all accrued leave in accordance with paragraph (a.), above, or the faculty member elects not to use accrued leave.

(3) This period of leave with or without pay shall be in accordance with Chapter 440 (Worker's Compensation), Florida Statutes.

(4) If, at the end of the leave period, the faculty member is unable to return to work and perform assigned duties, the President or representative should advise the faculty member, as appropriate, of the Florida Retirement System's disability provisions and application process, and may, based upon a current medical certification by a health care provider prescribed in accordance with Chapter 440 (Worker's Compensation), Florida Statutes, and taking the

University's needs into account:

    a. offer the faculty member part-time employment;

    b. place the faculty member in leave without pay status or extend such status;

    c. request the faculty member's resignation; or

    d. release the faculty member from employment, notwithstanding any other provisions of this Agreement.

(c) Compulsory Leave.

(1) Placing Faculty Members on Compulsory Leave.

    a. If a faculty member is unable to perform assigned duties due to illness/injury the President or representative may require the faculty member to submit to a medical examination, the results of which shall be released to the University, by a health care provider chosen and paid by the University or by a health care provider chosen and paid by the faculty member, who is acceptable to the President or representative. Such health care provider shall submit the appropriate medical certification(s) to the University.

    b. If the University agrees to accept the faculty member's choice of a health care provider the University may not then require another University-paid examination.

    c. If the medical examination confirms that the faculty member is unable to perform assigned duties, the President or representative shall place the faculty member on compulsory leave.

(2) Conditions of Compulsory Leave.

    a. Written notification to the faculty member placing the faculty member on compulsory leave shall include the duration of the compulsory leave period and the conditions under which the faculty member may return to work. These conditions may include the requirement of the successful completion of, or participation in, a program of rehabilitation or treatment, and follow-up medical certification(s) by the health care provider, as appropriate.

    b. The compulsory leave period may be leave with pay or leave without pay. If the compulsory leave combines the use of accrued leave with leave without pay, the use of such leave shall be in accordance with Section 17.11(e).

    c. If the faculty member fulfills the terms and conditions of the compulsory leave and receives a current medical certification that the faculty member is able to perform assigned duties, the President or representative shall return the faculty member to the faculty member's previous duties, if possible, or to equivalent duties.

(3) Duration. Compulsory leave, with or without pay, shall be for a period not to exceed the duration of the illness/injury or one year, whichever is less.

(4) Failure to Complete Conditions of Compulsory Leave or Inability to Return to Work. If the faculty member fails to fulfill the terms and conditions of a compulsory leave and/or is unable to return to work and perform assigned duties at the end of a leave period, the President or representative should advise the faculty member, as appropriate, of the Florida Retirement System's disability provisions and application process, and may, based upon the University's needs:

    a. offer the faculty member part-time employment;

b. place the faculty member in leave without pay status in accordance with Section 17.11 or extend such status;

c. request the faculty member's resignation; or

d. release the faculty member from employment, notwithstanding any other provisions of this Agreement.

17.9 Annual Leave.

(a) Accrual of Annual Leave.

(1) Full-time, salaried faculty members holding 12-month appointments shall accrue annual leave at the rate of 6.769 hours biweekly or 14.667 hours per month (or a number of hours that is directly proportionate to the number of days worked during less than a full-pay period for full-time faculty members), and the hours accrued shall be credited at the conclusion of each pay period or, upon termination, at the effective date of termination. Faculty members may accrue annual leave in excess of the year-end maximum during a calendar year. Faculty members with accrued annual leave in excess of the year-end maximum as of December 31 shall have any excess converted to post October 1, 1973 sick leave on an hour-for-hour basis on January 1 of each year.

(2) Part-time, salaried faculty members holding 12-month appointments shall accrue annual leave at a rate directly proportionate to the percent of time employed.

(3) Academic year faculty members (9-month faculty members) and OPS faculty members shall not accrue annual leave.

(b) Use and Transfer of Annual Leave.

(1) Annual leave shall be accrued before being taken, except in those instances where the President or representative may authorize the advancing of annual leave. When leave has been advanced and employment is terminated prior to the faculty member accruing sufficient annual leave to credit against the leave that was advanced, the state shall deduct from the faculty member's warrant the cost of any annual leave advanced under this provision. All requests for annual leave shall be submitted by the faculty member to the supervisor as far in advance as possible and appropriate. Approval of the dates on which a faculty member wishes to take annual leave shall be at the discretion of the supervisor and shall be subject to the consideration of departmental/unit and organizational scheduling. Faculty members shall be provided reasonable opportunity to utilize their annual leave during the course of the year.

(2) When a faculty member moves from a position in a governmental entity (state agency, university, community college, county or city) within Florida to an annual leave accruing position within the University, eighty (80) hours, or more with the approval of the hiring department/unit, of unused annual leave accrued in the classification and pay plan in which the faculty member was previously employed and for which payment was not made may accompany the faculty member; however, no more than thirty-one (31) days may elapse between jobs.

(3) A faculty member may transfer into an annual leave-accruing position up to forty-four (44) days of unused leave accrued in the University classification and pay plan in which

previously employed, provided the faculty member has not received payment for such leave and no more than thirty-one (31) days have elapsed between jobs.

(4) When an annual leave-accruing faculty member moves to a position within the SUS or in state government, the transfer of leave shall be governed by the rules of the plan to which the faculty member is transferring. Should all unused leave not be transferable, up to forty-four days (352 hours) of the remaining balance shall be paid in lump sum, effective the last day of University employment, without affecting other leave benefits.

(c) Payment for Unused Annual Leave.

(1) Upon termination from an annual leave-accruing contract, or transfer from an annual leave-accruing contract to an academic year and unless the faculty member requests the option in (2) below, the University shall pay the faculty member for up to forty-four days (352 hours) of unused annual leave at the calendar-year rate the faculty member was accruing as of the faculty member's last day of work, provided that a determination has been made by the President or representative that the faculty member was unable to reduce the unused annual leave balance prior to termination or reassignment to an academic year. All unused annual leave in excess of forty-four days (352 hours) shall be forfeited by the faculty member.

(2) Upon transfer from an annual leave-accruing contract to an academic year the faculty member may elect to retain all unused annual leave until such time, not to exceed two (2) years, as the faculty member transfers back to an annual leave-accruing contract or terminates employment with the University. Upon such termination or at the end of two (2) years, whichever comes first, the unused leave balance shall be paid in lump sum for up to forty-four days (352 hours) at the annual rate the faculty member was accruing as of the faculty member's last day of work on an annual leave-accruing contract.

(3) Upon layoff, a faculty member shall be paid for up to forty-four days (352 hours) of unused annual leave in lump sum, unless the faculty member requests in writing that annual leave credits be retained pending re-employment. For faculty members who are re-employed by the University within twelve (12) calendar months following layoff, all unused annual leave shall be restored to the faculty member, provided the faculty member requests such action in writing and repays the full amount of any lump sum leave payment received at the time of layoff. Faculty members who are not re-employed within twelve (12) calendar months following layoff and who elected to retain their annual leave pending re-employment shall be paid for up to forty-four days (352 hours) of unused annual leave at the calendar rate the faculty member was accruing as of the faculty member's last day of work.

(4) If a faculty member has received a lump sum payment for accrued annual leave, the faculty member may elect in writing, upon re-employment within 100 days, to restore the faculty member's accrued annual leave. Restoration will be effective upon the repayment of the full lump sum leave payment.

(5) In the event of the death of a faculty member, payment for all unused annual leave at the time of death, up to 352 hours, shall be made to the faculty member's beneficiary, estate, or as provided by law.

Article 17
LEAVES

17.10   Administrative Leaves.
    (a) Jury Duty and Court Appearances.
        (1) A faculty member who is summoned as a member of a jury panel or subpoenaed as a witness in a matter not involving the faculty member's personal interests, shall be granted leave with pay and any jury or witness fees shall be retained by the faculty member; leave granted hereunder shall not affect a faculty member's annual or sick leave balance.
        (2) An appearance as an expert witness for which a faculty member receives professional compensation falls under Article 19 and the University policies and rules relative to outside employment/conflict of interest. Such an appearance may necessitate the faculty member requesting annual leave or, if a non-annual leave-accruing employee, may necessitate the faculty member seeking an adjustment of the work schedule.
        (3) If a faculty member is required, as a direct result of the faculty member's employment, to appear as an official witness to testify in the course of any action as defined in Section 92.142(2), Florida Statutes, such duty shall be considered a part of the faculty member's job assignment, and the faculty member shall be paid per diem and travel expenses and shall turn over to the University any fees received.
        (4) A faculty member involved in personal litigation during work hours must request annual leave or, if a non-annual leave-accruing employee, must seek an adjustment to the work schedule.

    (b) Leave Pending Investigation. When the President or representative has reason to believe that the faculty member's presence on the job will adversely affect the operation of the University, the President or representative may immediately place the faculty member on leave pending investigation of the event(s) leading to that belief. The leave pending investigation shall commence immediately upon the President or representative providing the faculty member with a written notice of the reasons therefore. The leave shall be with pay, with no reduction of accrued leave.

    (c) Other Leaves Provided Not Affecting Accrued Leave Balances. A faculty member may be granted other leaves not affecting accrued leave balances which are provided as follows:
        (1) Florida Disaster Volunteer Leave is provided by Section 110.120, Florida Statutes, for a faculty member who is a certified disaster service volunteer of the American Red Cross. Leave of absence with pay for not more than fifteen (15) working days in the fiscal year may be provided upon request of the American Red Cross and the faculty member's supervisor's approval. Leave granted under this act shall be only for services related to a disaster occurring within the boundaries of the State of Florida.
        (2) Civil disorder or disaster leave is provided for a faculty member who is a member of a volunteer fire department, police auxiliary or reserve, civil defense unit, or other law enforcement type organization to perform duties in time of civil disturbances, riots, and natural disasters, including a faculty member who is a member of the Civil Air Patrol or Coast Guard Auxiliary, and called upon to assist in emergency search and rescue missions. Such paid leave not affecting leave balances may be granted upon approval by the President or designee and shall

not exceed two days on any one occasion.

(3) Athletic competition leave is provided by Section 110.118, Florida Statutes, for a faculty member who is a group leader, coach, official, or athlete who is a member of the official delegation of the United States team for athletic competition. Such paid leave not affecting leave balances shall be granted for the purpose of preparing for and engaging in the competition for the period of the official training camp and competition, not to exceed 30 days in a calendar year.

(4) Leave for re-examination or treatment with respect to service-connected disability is provided by Section 110.119, Florida Statues, for a faculty member who has such rating by the United State Department of Veterans Affairs and has been scheduled to be reexamined or treated for the disability. Upon presentation of written confirmation of having been so scheduled, such leave not affecting the faculty member's leave balances shall be approved and shall not exceed six (6) calendar days in any calendar year.

(d) Official Emergency Closings. The President or President's representative may close the University, or portions of the University, in the event an Executive Order declaring an emergency has been issued. When natural disasters or other sudden and unplanned emergency conditions occur which are not covered by an Executive Order, the President or representative shall determine whether the University, or any portion thereof, is affected by the emergency and is to be closed. Such closings will be only for the period it takes to restore normal working conditions. Leave resulting from such an emergency closing shall not reduce faculty members' leave balances.

(e) Bereavement Leave.

(1) In the event of a death in the immediate family of a faculty member, the faculty member is entitled to two (2) days paid bereavement leave to attend to necessary arrangements and appropriate observances.

(2) Nothing in this article is intended to preclude faculty members from exercising additional leave rights provided elsewhere in this article, including the use of unpaid leave, in association with bereavement.

17.11 Military Leave. Leave shall be granted in accordance with the provisions of this section upon presentation of a copy of the faculty member's official orders or appropriate military certification.

(a) Short-term Military Training. A faculty member who is a member of the United States Armed Forces Reserve, including the National Guard, shall be granted leave with pay during periods in which the faculty member is engaged in annual field training or other active or inactive duty for training exercises. Such leave with pay shall not exceed 240 hours in any one (1) federal fiscal year (October 1 - September 30).

(b) National Guard State Service. A faculty member who is a member of the Florida National Guard shall be granted leave with pay on all days when ordered to active service by the state. Such leave with pay shall not exceed thirty (30) days at any one time.

(c) Other Military Leave.

(1) A faculty member, except one who is employed in a temporary position or employed on a temporary basis, who is drafted, who volunteers for active military service, or who is ordered to active duty (not active duty training) shall be granted leave in accordance with Chapter 43 of Title 38, United States Code. Active military service includes active duty with any branch of the United States Army, Air Force, Navy, Marine Corps, Coast Guard, National Guard of the State of Florida, or other service as provided in Sections 115.08 and 115.09, Florida Statutes.

(2) Such leave of absence shall be verified by official orders or appropriate military certification. The first thirty (30) days of such leave shall be with full pay and shall not affect a faculty member's annual or sick leave balance. The remainder of military leave shall be without pay unless the faculty member elects to use accumulated annual leave or appropriate leave as provided in 17.11(c)(4) below, or the employer exercises its option under Section 115.14, Florida Statutes, to supplement the faculty member's military pay. Leave payment for the first thirty (30) days shall be made only upon receipt of evidence from appropriate military authority that thirty (30) days of military service have been completed.

(3) Applicable provisions of federal and state law shall govern the granting of military leave and the faculty member's re-employment rights.

(4) Use of accrued leave is authorized during a military leave without pay in accordance with Section 17.12.

17.12 Leave Without Pay.

(a) Granting. Upon request of a faculty member, the President or representative shall grant a leave without pay for a period not to exceed one year unless the President or representative determines that granting such leave would be inconsistent with the best interests of the University. Such leave may be extended upon mutual agreement.

(b) Salary Adjustment. The salary of a faculty member returning from uncompensated leave shall be adjusted to reflect all non-discretionary increases distributed during the period of leave. While on such leave, a faculty member shall be eligible to participate in any special salary incentive programs such as the Teaching Incentive Program.

(c) Retirement Credit. Retirement credit for such periods of leave without pay shall be governed by the rules and regulations of the Division of Retirement and the provisions of Chapter 121, Florida Statutes.

(d) Accrual of Leave/Holiday Pay. While on leave without pay, the faculty member shall retain accumulated sick leave and annual leave, but shall not accrue sick leave or annual leave nor be entitled to holiday pay.

(e) Use of Accrued Leave During an Approved Period of Leave Without Pay.

(1) Use of accrued leave with pay is authorized during a leave of absence without pay for parental, foster care, medical, or military reasons. Such use of leave with pay is provided under

the following conditions:

a. Notwithstanding the provisions of Section 17.8(a)(2) regarding the use of sick leave, a faculty member may use any type of accrued leave in an amount necessary to cover the faculty member's contribution to the state insurance program and other expenses incurred by the faculty member during an approved period of leave without pay for parental, foster care, medical, or military reasons.

b. Normally the use of accrued leave during a period of leave without pay for medical reasons shall be approved for up to six (6) months, but may be approved for up to one year for the serious health condition of the faculty member or a member of the faculty member's immediate family.

c. The employer contribution to the state insurance program will continue for the corresponding payroll periods.

(2) A faculty member's request for the use of accrued leave during a period of leave without pay shall be made at the time of the faculty member's request for the leave without pay. Such request shall include the amount of accrued leave the faculty member wishes to use during the approved period of leave without pay. If circumstances arise during the approved leave which cause the faculty member to reconsider the combination of leave with and without pay, the faculty member may request approval of revisions to the original approval.

Article 18
INVENTIONS AND WORKS

18.1   University Authority and Responsibilities. Section 1001.74, Florida
Statutes, authorizes the University to establish rules and procedures regarding patents, copyrights, and trademarks. Such rules and procedures shall be consistent with the terms of this Article.

18.2   Definitions. The following definitions shall apply in Article 18:

(a) A "work" includes any copyrightable material, such as printed material, computer software or databases, audio and visual material, circuit diagrams, architectural and engineering drawings, lectures, musical or dramatic compositions, choreographic works, pictorial or graphic works, and sculptural works.

(b) An "invention" includes any discovery, invention, process, composition of matter, article of manufacture, know-how, design, model, technological development, strain, variety, culture of any organism, or portion, modification, translation, or extension of these items, and any mark used in connection with these items.

(c) "University support" includes the use of University funds, personnel, facilities, equipment, materials, or technological information, and includes such support provided by other public or private organizations when it is arranged, administered, or controlled by the University.

18.3   Works.

Article 18
INVENTIONS AND WORKS

(a) Independent Efforts. A work made in the course of independent efforts is the property of the faculty member, who has the right to determine the disposition of such work and the revenue derived from such work. As used in this Section, the term "independent efforts" means that:

(1) the ideas came from the faculty member;

(2) the work was not University supported; and

(3) the University shall not be held responsible for any opinions expressed in the work.

(b) University-Supported Efforts.

(1) If the work was not made in the course of independent efforts, it is the property of the University and the faculty member shall share in the proceeds therefrom.

(2) Exceptions. The University shall not assert rights to the following works:

a. Those works for which the intended purpose is to disseminate the results of academic research, scholarly study, or creative efforts, such as books, articles, electronic media, databases, poems, musical compositions, and works of art, and

b. Software released by a faculty member to the academic and research community for general public use under a license, such as the Gnu General Public License, that provides it not be marketed for profit, and

c. Works developed without the use of appreciable University support and used solely for the purpose of assisting or enhancing the faculty member's instructional assignment. Examples of such works include case studies, text books, laboratory manuals and class notes produced in connection with regularly scheduled courses of instruction, regardless of the medium. For University support to be appreciable it must go beyond the resources commonly or routinely provided or made available to similarly situated faculty members for the performance of the instructional assignment. For example, the use of resources such as the libraries; one's office, office computer and other University computer facilities; and office supplies is not considered appreciable University support.

(c) Disclosure.

(1) Upon the creation of a work and prior to any publication, the faculty member shall disclose to the President or representative any work made in the course of University-supported efforts, together with an outline of the project and the conditions under which it was done. Faculty members need not disclose regarding works covered by 18.3(b)(2) (Exceptions), above.

(2) The President or representative shall assess the relative equities of the faculty member and the University in the work.

(3) Within sixty (60) days after such disclosure, the President or representative will inform the faculty member whether the University seeks an interest in the work, and a written agreement shall thereafter be negotiated to reflect the interests of both parties, including provisions relating to the equities of the faculty member and the allocation of proceeds resulting from such work. Creation, use, and revision of such works shall also be the subject of the written agreement between the faculty member and the University as well as provisions relating to the use or revision of such works by persons other than the author. The faculty member shall assist the University in obtaining releases from persons appearing in, or giving financial or creative

support to, the development or use of these works in which the University has an interest. All such agreements shall comport with and satisfy any preexisting commitments to outside sponsoring contractors.

(4) The faculty member and the University shall not commit any act which would tend to defeat the University's or faculty member's interest in the work and shall take any necessary steps to protect such interests.

18.4   Inventions.

(a) Disclosure/University Review.

(1) A faculty member shall fully and completely disclose to the President or representative all inventions which the faculty member develops or discovers while an employee of the University, together with an outline of the project and the conditions under which it was done. With respect to inventions made during the course of approved outside employment, the faculty member may delay such disclosure, when necessary to protect the outside employer's interests, until the decision has been made by the outside employer whether to seek a patent.

(2) If the University wishes to assert its interest in the invention, the President or representative shall inform the faculty member within 120 days of the faculty member's disclosure to the President or representative.

(3) The President or representative shall conduct an investigation which shall assess the respective equities of the faculty member and the University in the invention, and determine its importance and the extent to which the University should be involved in its protection, development, and promotion.

(4) The President or representative shall inform the faculty member of the University's decision regarding the University's interest in the invention within a reasonable time, not to exceed 135 days from the date of the disclosure to the President or representative.

(5) The division, between the University and the faculty member, of proceeds generated by the licensing or assignment of an invention shall be negotiated and reflected in a written contract between the University and the faculty member. All such agreements shall comport with and satisfy any preexisting commitments to outside sponsoring contractors.

(6) The faculty member shall not commit any act which would tend to defeat the University's interest in the matter, and the University shall take any necessary steps to protect such interest.

(b) Independent Efforts. All inventions made outside the field or discipline in which the faculty member is employed by the University and for which no University support has been used are the property of the faculty member, who has the right to determine the disposition of such work and revenue derived from such work. The faculty member and the President or representative may agree that the patent for such invention be pursued by the University and the proceeds shared.

(c) University-Supported Efforts. An invention which is made in the field or discipline in which the faculty member is employed by the University, or by using University support, is the property of the University and the faculty member shall share in the proceeds therefrom.

(d) Release of Rights.

(1) In the event a sponsored research contractor has been offered the option to apply for the patent to an invention or other rights in an invention, the University will use its good offices in an effort to obtain the contractor's decision regarding the exercise of such rights within 120 days.

(2) At any stage of making the patent applications, or in the commercial application of an invention, if it has not otherwise assigned to a third party the right to pursue its interests, the President or representative may elect to withdraw from further involvement in the protection or commercial application of the invention. At the request of the faculty member in such case, the University shall transfer the invention rights to the faculty member, in which case the invention shall be the faculty member's property and none of the costs incurred by the University or on its behalf shall be assessed against the faculty member.

(3) All assignments or releases of inventions, including patent rights, by the President or representative to the faculty member shall contain the provision that such invention, if patented by the faculty member, shall be available royalty-free for governmental purposes of the State of Florida, unless otherwise agreed in writing by the University.

(e) University Policy.

(1) The University shall have a policy addressing the division of proceeds between the faculty member and the University.

(2) Division of Proceeds. When a U.S. patent is issued on an invention assigned to the University, the inventor will receive a $500 payment.

a.   The first $10,000 of royalties or other income resulting from inventions in which the University takes title will be distributed as follows:

85% to the inventor(s)
15% to the University.

b.   Once the $10,000 plateau has been reached, net income (gross royalties minus direct costs of patenting, licensing, legal, and other related expenses) in excess of $10,000 will be divided as follows:

40% to the inventor(s)
30% to the department/ unit of which the inventor is a member
30% to the University.

(3) Other aspects of such policy may be the subject of consultation meetings pursuant to Article 2.

(f) Execution of Documents. The University and the faculty member shall sign an agreement individually recognizing the terms of this Article.

18.5   Outside Activity.

(a) Although a faculty member may, in accordance with Article 19, Conflict of Interest/Outside Activity, engage in outside activity, including employment, pursuant to a consulting agreement, requirements that a faculty member waive the faculty member's or University's rights to any work or inventions which arise during the course of such outside activity must be approved by the President or representative.

(b) A faculty member who proposes to engage in such outside activity shall furnish a copy of this Article and the University's patents policy to the outside employer prior to or at the time a consulting or other agreement is signed, or if there is no written agreement, before the employment begins.

18.6   Additional Faculty Interests in University-Supported Educational Materials.

(a) "Educational materials" are works developed for the purpose of instruction.

(b) The University shall not claim ownership of educational materials created by a faculty member unless

(1) The creator has employed in its development, without personal charge to him/herself, the equipment, materials or staff services of one or more of the organizations established or supported by the University primarily to assist in developing and producing educational materials; or

(2) The creator has been both commissioned in writing by the University, or one of its colleges, schools, departments or other subdivisions, to develop the work and, in its production has received assistance in the forms of release time and/or University funds, including grants and contract funds administered by the University.

(c) Creative Control. Subject to the provisions of this agreement, the creator has the right to and the responsibility for control of the content and the right to make other versions of the content of the materials for presentation in other media.

(d) Internal Use.

(1) Use of University-supported educational materials within the University requires approval of the creator.

(2) As long as the creator of University-supported educational materials remains an employee of the University, he or she has the right to revise any or all materials because of obsolescence provided that the University shall not be obligated to provide further resources for the development of any such revisions unless the revisions are requested by the University or agreed upon jointly by the University and the creator. Should the extent of the required revision exceed the resources of University supporting agencies involved, materials may be withdrawn by agreement of the creator and the University.

(3) If the University-supported educational materials are used internally without revision for a period of two years, the University shall request the creator and the appropriate University supporting agency or agencies to consider revising the materials or to determine whether they

shall continue to be used.

(4) The creator has the right to make personal and professional use of the materials within the University. Scheduling and arrangements to cover the costs for such personal requests will be made with the University supporting services involved with the original production of the educational materials.

(5) If the creator terminates employment with the University, the University retains the right to continued internal use of the University-supported educational materials in accordance with this policy unless special conditions for subsequent internal use have been arrived at by joint written agreement of the creator and the University.

(6) The creator has the right to use the University-supported educational materials at no cost to the University after termination of his or her employment with the University subject to the provisions of this policy.

(e) External Use. Licensing or sale or publication of University-supported educational materials for external use shall be preceded by a written agreement between the University and the creator specifying the conditions or use, including provisions concerning the right of the creator to revise the materials or to withdraw them from use, and the distribution of net royalty income.

(f) Compensation for Production Activity.

(1) With the exception of payments made by dual compensation appointments, the University shall not make any payment to the creator of University-supported educational materials other than the compensation regularly received.

(2) The regular assignment of the creator may be adjusted to take into account the extra time required to develop, or produce, or revise the University-supported educational materials.

(3) The creator may receive payment for the development of materials. Such additive compensation will be provided for in a written agreement between the University and the creator.

(g) Distribution of Royalties.

(1) The University shall license the external use of University-supported materials only after it enters into a written agreement with the creator specifying the distribution of net royalty income.

(2) Such an agreement will be subject to the following guidelines:

a. The University's original production costs shall be recovered by the University prior to the distribution of any royalties. Production costs will include the following categories:

i. Direct costs. Those salaries and materials specifically identified with the production of such materials. Direct costs are computed by those supporting agencies involved with design, preparation, production, editing, duplication and distribution of the work.

ii. Indirect costs (Overhead). Costs for space, utilities, amortization of equipment, etc., which are generally referred to as overhead. The current University indirect cost rate will be applied for recovery of indirect costs relating to the production of University-supported works.

b. Expenses related to the production and distribution of additional copies of educational materials will be recovered from each sale or rental on the same basis as the original production costs.

c. Royalties may be included in the sale or rental price subject to any limitation imposed by outside contracting or granting agencies.

d. Fifty percent of any resultant net royalty income (royalty income after production costs and distribution costs) derived from the external use of University-supported educational materials will go to the University, and fifty percent to the creator.

e. Twenty-five percent of the University's share shall be allocated to SRAD. The remaining royalties that accrue to the University shall be returned to the school, college and/or supporting agency to finance further the development of educational materials or for other educational purposes. Distribution shall be as negotiated among the Vice President, Research and Graduate Studies, and the chief administrator of the department, school, college or agency involved.

Article 19
CONFLICT OF INTEREST/OUTSIDE ACTIVITY

19.1   Policy.

(a) A faculty member is bound to observe, in all official acts, the highest standards of ethics consistent with the code of ethics of the State of Florida (Chapter 112, Part III, Florida Statutes), the advisory opinions rendered with respect thereto, and University rules.

(b) Nothing in this Article is intended to discourage a faculty member from engaging in outside activity in order to increase the faculty member's professional reputation, service to the community, or income, subject to the conditions stated herein.

19.2   Definitions.

(a) "Outside Activity" shall mean any private practice, private consulting, additional teaching or research, or other activity, compensated or uncompensated, which is not part of the faculty member's assigned duties and for which the University has provided no compensation.

(b) "Conflict of Interest" shall mean

(1) any conflict between the private interests of the faculty member and the public interests of the University, or the State of Florida, including conflicts of interest specified under Florida Statutes; or

(2) any activity which interferes with the full performance of the faculty member's professional or institutional responsibilities or obligations.

19.3   Conflicts of Interest Prohibited. Conflicts of interest, including those arising from University or outside activities, are prohibited. Faculty members are responsible for resolving such conflicts of interest, working in conjunction with their supervisors and other University officials.

Article 19
CONFLICT OF INTEREST/OUTSIDE ACTIVITY

19.4   Report and Approval of Outside Activity.

(a) A faculty member who proposes to engage in any outside activity which the faculty member should reasonably conclude may create a conflict of interest, or in any outside compensated professional activity, shall report to the faculty member's supervisor, in writing, the details of such proposed activity prior to engaging therein.

(b) The report, as described in paragraph 19.4(a) shall include where applicable, the name of the employer or other recipient of services; the funding source; the location where such activity shall be performed; the nature and extent of the activity; and any intended use of University facilities, equipment, or services.

(c) A new report shall be submitted for outside activity previously reported at:
    (1) the beginning of each academic year for outside activity of a continuing nature; and
    (2) such time as there is a significant change in an activity (nature, extent, funding, etc.)

(d) A faculty member may assume tacit approval unless written disapproval is issued prior to the reported starting date. If it is later determined that the activity represents a conflict of interest, the faculty member must cease the activity, except as provided in 19.5 (b).

(e) Any outside activity that falls under the provisions of this Article and in which the faculty member is currently engaged but has not previously reported, shall be reported within sixty (60) days of the execution of this Agreement and shall conform to the provisions of this Article.

19.5   Rights to the Expedited Grievance Procedure.

(a) In the event the proposed outside activity is determined to constitute a conflict of interest, and the faculty member disagrees with that determination the faculty member may file a grievance under the expedited grievance procedure contained in Article 20. Alternatively, the faculty member may, within seven (7) days, seek a review in writing by the University Review Committee on Outside Activities and Conflict of Interest, or a subcommittee of at least three faculty members thereof, for an advisory opinion, unless the Committee has been consulted previously on this matter. The Committee shall render its opinion in writing within 7 days of receipt of the faculty member's request. If the Committee concludes that the outside activity could have been approved, it shall consult with the approving authority to seek resolution of the matter. Should satisfactory resolution not be attained, the Committee may recommend to the President that the activity be approved. If no resolution is attained within fourteen (14) days from the date the faculty member receives the written opinion of the Committee, the faculty member may file a grievance under the expedited grievance procedure contained in Article 20.

(b) The faculty member may engage in such outside activity pending a resolution of the matter pursuant to Section 19.5(a).

(c) If the resolution of the matter is that there is a conflict of interest, the faculty member shall cease such activity immediately and may be required to turn over to the University all or part of compensation earned therefrom.

19.6 Use of University Resources. A faculty member engaging in any outside activity shall not use the facilities, equipment, or services of the University in connection with such outside activity without prior approval of the President or representative. Approval for the use of University facilities, equipment, or services may be conditioned upon reimbursement for the use thereof.

19.7 No University Affiliation. A faculty member engaging in outside activity shall take reasonable precautions to ensure that the outside employer or other recipient of services understands that the faculty member is engaging in such outside activity as a private citizen and not as an employee, agent, or spokesperson of the University.

19.8 Relationships with students. Sexual relationships between faculty members and students where a direct supervisory or evaluative relationship exists are fraught with the potential for exploitation. The respect and trust accorded a faculty member by a student, as well as the power exercised by the faculty member in a direct supervisory or evaluative role, make voluntary consent by the student suspect. In their relationships with students, faculty members are expected to be aware of their professional responsibilities and to avoid conflict of interest, favoritism, or bias.

(a) When any direct supervisory or evaluative role exists, a consensual sexual relationship between a student and a faculty member is a conflict of interest.

(b) Any situation of direct supervision or evaluation will be ended immediately when a consensual sexual relationship between a student and a faculty member exists.

(c) Any such relationship must be disclosed to the faculty member's supervisor immediately.

(d) Direct supervision includes any type of evaluative role. Examples of direct supervision of the student include teaching the student's class, serving as a thesis or dissertation director, instructor of record, member of the student's thesis or dissertation committee, member of the student's comprehensive or doctoral exam committee, member of other committees where the focus is evaluation or supervision of the student's academic competence or the student's assistantship.

Article 20
GRIEVANCE PROCEDURE AND ARBITRATION

20.1 Policy/Informal Resolution. The purpose of this article is to promote a prompt and efficient procedure for the investigation and resolution of grievances. The procedures hereinafter set forth shall be the sole and exclusive method for resolving the grievances of faculty members as defined herein. The parties agree that all problems should be resolved, whenever possible, before the filing of a grievance but within the time limits for filing grievances stated elsewhere in this article, and encourage open communications between administrators and faculty members so that resorting to the formal grievance procedure will not normally be necessary. The parties further encourage the informal resolution of grievances whenever possible. At each step in the grievance process, participants are encouraged to pursue appropriate modes of conflict resolution including the use of mediation.

20.2   Resort to Other Procedures. It is the intent of the parties to first provide a reasonable opportunity for resolution of a dispute through the grievance procedure and arbitration process. Except as noted below, if prior to seeking resolution of a dispute by filing a grievance hereunder, or while the grievance proceeding is in progress, a faculty member requests, in writing, resolution of the matter in any other forum, whether administrative or judicial, the Board or the University shall have no obligation to entertain or proceed further with the matter pursuant to this grievance procedure. As an exception to this provision, a grievant may file an EEOC charge while the grievance is in progress when such filing becomes necessary to meet federal filing deadlines pursuant to 42 U.S.C. § 2000e et seq. Further, since the parties do not intend that this grievance procedure be a device for appellate review, the President's response to a recommendation of a hearing officer or other individual or group having appropriate jurisdiction in any other procedure shall not be an act or omission giving rise to a grievance under this procedure.

20.3   Definitions and Forms. As used herein:
   (a) The term "grievance" shall mean a dispute filed on a form referenced in Section 20.3(c) concerning the interpretation or application of a specific term or provision of this Agreement, subject to those exclusions appearing in other Articles of this Agreement.

   (b) The term "grievant" shall mean:
         (1) a faculty member or group of faculty members who has/have filed a grievance in a dispute over a provision of this Agreement which confers rights upon the faculty member(s);
         (2) the UFF where it has filed a grievance without the aggrieved faculty member(s) in a dispute over a provision of this agreement which confers rights upon such faculty members(s); or
         (3) the UFF where it has filed a grievance in a dispute over a provision of this Agreement which confers rights upon the UFF. A grievance filed by the FSU Chapter of the UFF which alleges a violation of its rights by the University may be initiated at Step 2. A grievance of a decision made by the President or the Provost is to be initiated at Step 2. The parties may agree to consolidate grievances of a similar nature to expedite the review process.

   (c) Grievance Forms. Each grievance, request for review, and notice of arbitration must be submitted in writing on the appropriate form attached to this Agreement as Appendix "C", "D", or "E", respectively, and shall be signed by the grievant. All grievance forms shall be dated when the grievance is received. If there is difficulty in meeting any time limit, the UFF representative may sign such documents for the grievant; however, grievant's signature shall be provided prior to the Step 1 meeting or Step 2 meeting if filed directly at Step 2. The aforementioned grievance forms, as well as Appendix "H", may be filed by means of fax, United States mail, or any other recognized means of delivery.

20.4   Burden of Proof. In all grievances except disciplinary grievances in accordance with Article 16, Disciplinary Action and Job Abandonment and any other exceptions stated elsewhere in this Agreement, the burden of proof shall be on the faculty member. In disciplinary grievances, the burden of proof shall be on the Board.

20.5   Representation. The UFF shall have the exclusive right to represent any faculty member in a grievance filed hereunder, unless a faculty member elects self-representation or to be represented by legal counsel. If a faculty member elects not to be represented by the UFF, the University shall promptly inform the UFF in writing of the grievance. No resolution of any individually processed grievance shall be inconsistent with the terms of this Agreement and for this purpose the UFF shall have the right to have an observer present at all meetings called for the purpose of discussing such grievance. The UFF Grievance Chair or representative shall be informed of the dates and times of any such meetings at the same time as the other parties. The UFF Grievance Chair shall be sent copies of all correspondence related to such, including grievance decisions at the same time as they are sent to the other parties.

20.6   Grievance Representatives. The UFF shall annually furnish to the Board a list of all persons authorized to act as grievance representatives and shall update the list as needed. The UFF grievance representative shall have the responsibility to meet all classes, office hours, and other duties and responsibilities incidental to the assigned workload. Some of these activities are scheduled to be performed at particular times. Such representative shall have the right during times outside of those hours scheduled for these activities to investigate, consult, and prepare grievance presentations and attend grievance hearings and meetings. Should any hearings or meetings with the dean or unit head, the provost, or their representatives necessitate rescheduling of assigned duties, the representative may, with the approval of the appropriate administrator, arrange for the rescheduling of such duties or their coverage by colleagues. Such approval shall not be unreasonably withheld.

20.7   Appearances.
    (a) When a faculty member participates in an arbitration hearing or in a grievance meeting between the grievant or representative and the Board or representative, that faculty member's compensation shall neither be reduced nor increased for time spent in those activities.

    (b) Prior to participation in any such proceedings, conferences, or meetings, the faculty member shall make arrangements acceptable to the appropriate supervisor for the performance of the faculty member's scheduled duties as defined in Article 9.1. Approval of such arrangements shall not be unreasonably withheld. Time spent in such activities outside regular working hours shall not be counted as time worked.

20.8   Formal Grievance Procedure.

(a) Facilitation. Consistent with the policy of informal resolution set forth in Section 20.1 of this Article, no grievance shall be considered ripe for filing at Step 1 absent submission of a request for facilitation. A request for facilitation shall be filed within forty-five (45) days of the date the faculty member learned of the alleged act or omission giving rise to the dispute (or the most recent in a series of alleged acts or omissions giving rise to the dispute). All requests for facilitation shall be in writing by the affected faculty member(s) or the UFF, as appropriate, and submitted to the Vice President for Faculty Development and Advancement or his/her designee. Such requests shall contain a general description of the potential dispute, including dates, times, and locations, along with copies of relevant documentation. Upon receipt of a request for facilitation, the Vice President for Faculty Development and Advancement and the UFF shall engage in a process of facilitation for a period of thirty (30) days, which may be modified by the parties' mutual agreement, in an effort to produce an informal resolution of the potential dispute. In matters designated in the request for facilitation as time-sensitive, the facilitation period shall be fifteen (15) days. Such fifteen (15) day facilitation period may be modified by the parties' mutual agreement in writing. All resolutions shall be reduced to writing, but shall be without precedent or prejudice to the parties.

(b) Filing.

(1) Within fifteen (15) days from the conclusion of a facilitation period that failed to produce an informal resolution, the grievant shall be entitled to file a Step 1 grievance with the unit head, defined for the purpose of this Article as dean or comparable-level administrator, as appropriate. The grievant may amend the Appendix "C" form up to and including Step 2 of the grievance procedure so long as the factual basis of the complaint is not materially altered.

(2) A faculty member may seek redress of alleged salary discrimination by filing a grievance under the provisions of Article 20. An act or omission giving rise to such a grievance may be the faculty member's receipt of the salary warrant for the first full-pay period in which the annual salary increases referenced in Article 23 are reflected

(3) The filing of a grievance constitutes a waiver of any rights to judicial review of agency action pursuant to Chapter 120, Florida Statutes, or to the review of such actions under University procedures that may otherwise be available to address such matters. This grievance procedure shall be the sole review mechanism for resolving disputes regarding rights or benefits that are provided exclusively by this Agreement. Except as otherwise provided herein, only those acts or omissions and sections of the Agreement identified at the initial filing may be considered at subsequent steps.

(c) Time Limits. All time limits contained in this Article may be extended by mutual agreement of the parties, except that the time limits for the initial filing of a grievance may be extended only by agreement between the University and the UFF. Upon failure of the Board to provide a decision within the time limits provided in this Article, the grievant or the UFF, where appropriate, may appeal to the next step. Upon the failure of the grievant or the UFF, where appropriate, to file an appeal within the time limits provided in this Article, the grievance shall be deemed to have been resolved by the decision at the prior step.

(d) Step 1.

(1) Meeting. The Unit Head or his/her representative and the grievant and the grievant's representative shall meet at a mutually convenient time within fifteen (15) days following receipt of the grievance. At the Step 1 meeting, the grievant shall have the right to present any evidence in support of the grievance, and the grievant and/or the UFF representative or the grievant's legal counsel (if selected pursuant to Section 20.5), and the Unit Head or representative, shall discuss the grievance.

(2) Decision. The Unit Head or representative shall issue a written decision, stating the reasons therefore, to grievant's Step 1 representative within fifteen (15) days following the conclusion of the meeting. Fifteen (15) days shall be determined by a receipt executed by the office receiving the grievance, or by the date of mailing as determined by the postmark. In the absence of an agreement to extend the period for issuing the Step 1 decision, the grievant may proceed to Step 2 if the grievant's Step 1 representative has not received the written decision by the end of the twentieth (20th) day following the conclusion of the Step 1 meeting. A copy of the decision shall be sent to the grievant and to the local UFF grievance representative if the grievant elected self-representation or representation by legal counsel.

(3) Documents. Where practicable, the Step 1 reviewer shall make available to the grievant, or grievance representative, documentation referenced in the Step 1 decision prior to its issuance. All documents referred to in the decision and any additional documents presented by the grievant shall be attached to the decision, together with a list of these documents. In advance of the Step 1 meeting, the grievant shall have the right, upon written request, to a copy of any identifiable documents relevant to the grievance.

(4) Step 1 Meeting Waiver. The Step 1 meeting may be waived by mutual written agreement between the Board and the UFF.

(e) Step 2.

(1) Review. If the grievance is not satisfactorily resolved at Step 1, the grievant may file a written request for review with the Provost or his/her representative within fifteen (15) days following receipt of the Step 1 decision by the grievant's Step 1 representative. Fifteen (15) days shall be determined by a receipt executed by the office receiving the grievance, or by the date of mailing as determined by the postmark.

(2) Meeting. The Provost or representative and the grievant and the grievant's representative shall meet at a mutually convenient date and time not later than fifteen (15) days following receipt of written notice of request for a Step 2 review. At the Step 2 meeting, the grievant shall have the right to present any evidence in support of the grievance, and the grievant and/or the UFF representative or the grievant's legal counsel (if selected pursuant to Section 20.5), and the Provost or representative, shall discuss the grievance.

(3) Decision. The Provost or his/her representative shall issue a written decision, stating the reasons therefore, to grievant's Step 2 representative within fifteen (15) days following the

conclusion of the review meeting. Fifteen (15) days shall be determined by a receipt executed by the office receiving the grievance, or by the date of mailing as determined by the postmark. In the absence of an agreement to extend the period for issuing the Step 2 decision, the UFF may proceed to Step 3 (arbitration) if the grievant's Step 2 representative has not received the written decision by the end of the twentieth (20th) day following the conclusion of the Step 2 meeting. A copy of the decision shall be sent to the grievant and to the UFF if the grievant elected self-representation or representation by legal counsel.

(4) Documents. The decision shall not refer to any documents other than those presented by the grievant and the Provost or representative at or prior to the Step 2 meeting, except by mutual written agreement of the grievant and the Provost or representative. Documents referred to in the decision and any additional documents presented by the grievant at or prior to the Step 2 meeting shall be attached to the decision unless such documents are public and readily available, together with a list of these documents.

(f) Step 3 Arbitration.

(1) Filing. If the grievance has not been satisfactorily resolved at Step 2, the UFF may, upon the request of the grievant, proceed to arbitration by filing a written notice of the intent to do so. Notice of intent to proceed to arbitration must be filed with the Office of the President within fifteen (15) days after receipt of the Step 2 decision by the grievant's Step 2 representative and shall be signed by the grievant and the state UFF President or representative, or state UFF Director of Arbitrations Fifteen (15) days shall be determined by a receipt executed by the office receiving the grievance, or by the date of mailing as determined by the postmark. The grievance may be withdrawn at any time by the grievant or by the UFF President or Director of Arbitrations at any point during Step 3. The parties shall stipulate to the issue(s) prior to the arbitration. In the event a stipulation is not reached, the parties shall proceed to a hearing on arbitrability pursuant to Section 20.8 (f)(4).

(2) Selection of Arbitrator. Representatives of the University and the UFF shall meet within ninety (90) days after the execution of this Agreement for the purpose of selecting an Arbitration Panel of no less than five (5) members. Within fifteen (15) days after receipt of a notice of intent to arbitrate, representatives of the University and the UFF shall meet for the purpose of selecting an arbitrator from the Panel. Selection shall be by mutual agreement or by alternately striking names from the Arbitration Panel list until one name remains. The right of the first choice to strike from the list shall be determined by the flip of a coin. If the parties are unable to agree to a panel of arbitrators, they shall follow the normal American Arbitration Association procedure for the selection of an arbitrator. The parties may mutually select as the arbitrator an individual who is not a member of the Arbitration Panel. The arbitration shall be held within sixty (60) days following the selection of the arbitrator.

(3) Authority of the Arbitrator.

a. The arbitrator shall neither add to, subtract from, modify, nor alter the terms or provisions of this Agreement. Arbitration shall be confined solely to the application and/or interpretation of this Agreement and the precise issue(s) submitted for arbitration. The arbitrator shall refrain from issuing any statements of opinion or conclusions not essential to the determination of the issues submitted.

b. Where an administrator has made a judgment involving the exercise of discretion, such as decisions regarding tenure or promotion, the arbitrator shall not substitute the arbitrator's judgment for that of the administrator. Nor shall the arbitrator review such decision except for the purpose of determining whether the decision has violated this Agreement. If the arbitrator determines that the Agreement has been violated, the arbitrator shall direct the University to take appropriate action that the arbitrator shall specify. An arbitrator may award back salary where the arbitrator determines that the faculty member is not receiving the appropriate salary from the University, and any other payments to which a faculty member is entitled by the provisions of this Agreement, but the arbitrator may not award other monetary damages or penalties. If notice that further employment will not be offered is not given on time, the arbitrator may direct the University to renew the appointment only upon a finding that no other remedy is adequate, and that the notice was given so late that (a) the faculty member was deprived of reasonable opportunity to seek other employment, or (b) the faculty member actually rejected an offer of comparable employment which the faculty member otherwise would have accepted.

c. An arbitrator's decision awarding employment beyond the sixth year shall not of itself entitle the faculty member to tenure. In such cases the faculty member shall serve during the seventh year without further right to notice that the faculty member will not be offered employment thereafter. If a faculty member is reappointed at the direction of an arbitrator, the President or representative may reassign the faculty member during such reappointment

(4) Arbitrability. Issues of arbitrability shall be bifurcated from the substantive issue(s) and, whenever possible, determined by means of a hearing conducted by conference call. The arbitrator shall have ten (10) days from the hearing to render a decision on arbitrability. If the issue is judged to be arbitrable, an arbitrator shall then be selected to hear the substantive issue(s) in accordance with the provisions of Section 20.8(f)(2).

(5) Conduct of Hearing. The arbitrator shall hold the hearing in Tallahassee, unless otherwise agreed by the parties. The hearing shall commence within sixty (60) days of the arbitrator's acceptance of selection and the arbitrator shall issue the decision within forty-five (45) days of the close of the hearing or the submission of briefs, whichever is later, unless additional time is agreed to by the parties. The decision shall be in writing and shall set forth findings of fact, reasoning, and conclusions on the issues submitted. Except as modified by the provisions of this Agreement, arbitration proceedings shall be conducted in accordance with the rules and procedures of the American Arbitration Association.

(6) Effect of Decision. The decision or award of the arbitrator shall be final and binding upon the University, the UFF, and the grievant, provided that either party may appeal such award to an appropriate court of law pursuant to the Florida Arbitration Code, Chapter 682, Florida Statutes.

(7) Venue. For purposes of venue in any judicial review of an arbitrator's decision issued under this agreement, the parties agree that such an appeal shall be filed in the courts in Leon County, Florida, unless both parties specifically agree otherwise in a particular instance. In an

action commenced in Leon County, neither the Board nor the UFF will move for a change of venue based upon the defendant's residence in fact if other than Leon County.

(8) Fees and Expenses. All fees and expenses of the arbitrator shall be divided equally between the parties. Each party shall bear the cost of preparing and presenting its own case. The party desiring a transcript of the arbitration proceedings shall provide written notice to the other party of its intention to have a transcript of the arbitration made at least one week prior to the date of the arbitration. The party desiring such transcript shall be responsible for scheduling a stenotype reporter to record the proceedings. The parties shall share equally the appearance fee of the stenotype reporter and the cost of obtaining an original transcript and one copy for the party originally requesting a transcript of the proceedings. The requesting party shall, at its expense, photocopy the copy of the transcript received from the reporter and deliver the photocopy to the other party within five days after receiving the copy of the transcript from the reporter.

(9) Retroactivity. An arbitrator's award may or may not be retroactive as the equities of each case may demand, but in no case shall an award be retroactive to a date earlier than thirty (30) days prior to the date the grievance was initially filed in accordance with this Article.

20.9   Filings and Notification. With the exception of Step 1 and Step 2 decisions, all documents required or permitted to be issued or filed pursuant to this Article may be transmitted by fax, United States mail, or any other recognized delivery service (note: e-mail is not an acceptable form of delivery). Step 1 and Step 2 decisions shall be transmitted to the grievant's representative(s) by personal delivery with written documentation of receipt or by certified mail, return receipt requested. In the event that any action falls due on a Saturday, Sunday, or holiday (as referred to in Section 17.5), the action will be considered timely if it is accomplished by 5:00 P.M. on the following business day.

20.10   Precedent. No complaint informally resolved, or grievance resolved at either Step 1 or 2, shall constitute a precedent for any purpose unless agreed to in writing by the Board of Trustees or representative and the UFF acting through its President or representative.

20.11   Processing.

(a) The filing or pendency of any grievance or arbitration proceedings under this Article shall not operate to impede, preclude, or delay the University from taking the action complained of. Reasonable efforts, including the shortening of time limits when practical, shall be made to conclude the processing of a grievance prior to the expiration of the grievant's employment, whether by termination or failure to reappoint. A faculty member with a pending grievance will not continue to be compensated beyond the last date of employment.

(b) Nothing herein shall be construed to authorize the Unit Head, the President, the Provost, or their representatives to refuse to respond to a grievance filed under this Article.

20.12   Reprisal. No reprisal of any kind will be made by the University or the UFF against any grievant, any witness, any UFF representative, or any other participant in the grievance procedure by reason of such participation. In a grievance where the arbitrator has established that the grievant has made a prima facie case of reprisal, the burden of proof shall be on the Board to demonstrate that there was no reprisal.

20.13   Records. All written materials pertinent to a grievance shall be filed separately from the evaluation file of the grievant or witnesses, except decisions resulting from arbitration or settlement.

20.14   Inactive Grievances. A grievance which has been filed at Step 2 or Step 3 and on which no action has been taken by the grievant or the UFF for sixty (60) days shall be deemed withdrawn and resolved in accordance with the decision issued at the prior Step.

20.15   Expedited Grievance Procedure for Conflict of Interest (Section 19.5).

(a) A grievance alleging a violation of Article 19 shall be heard at Step 1 by the President or representative no more than seven (7) days after it has been filed. The President or representative shall issue a Step 1 decision no more than 7 days after the Step 1 meeting.

(b) A request for review of the Step 1 decision shall be filed using Appendix "D", no more than seven (7) days following the receipt of the Step 1 decision. The Step 2 meeting shall be held no more than 7 days after the receipt of Appendix "D", and the Step 2 decision shall be issued no more than 7 days after the meeting.

(c) A request for arbitration using Appendix "E" shall be filed within fourteen (14) days after receipt of the Step 2 decision. An arbitrator shall be selected by the parties no more than fourteen (14) days following the receipt of the Appendix "E". The arbitrator shall issue a memorandum of decision within 7 days following the conclusion of the arbitration, to be followed by a written opinion and award in accordance with Section 20.8(f)(5).

(d) The parties shall establish a panel of three (3) experienced arbitrators to hear a grievance filed in accordance with this Section.

(e) All other provisions of Article 20 shall apply to these grievances, except as noted above.

Article 21
OTHER FACULTY RIGHTS

21.1   Professional Meetings. Faculty members should be encouraged to and may, with the approval of the supervisor, attend professional meetings, conferences, and activities. Subject to the availability of funds, the faculty member's expenses in connection with such meetings, conferences, or activities shall be reimbursed in accordance with the applicable provisions of state law and rules and regulations having the force and effect of law.

Article 21
OTHER FACULTY RIGHTS

21.2   Office Space. Each faculty member shall be provided with office space which may be on a shared basis. The parties recognize the desirability of providing each faculty member with enclosed office space with a door lock, office equipment commensurate with assigned responsibilities, and ready access to a telephone. Each faculty member shall, consistent with building security, have reasonable access to the faculty member's office space and laboratories, studios, music rooms, and the like used in connection with assigned responsibilities; this provision may require that campus security provide access on an individual basis. Before a faculty member's office location is changed, or before there is a substantial alteration to a faculty member's office to a degree that impedes the faculty member's work effectiveness, the affected faculty member shall be notified, if practicable, at least one (1) month prior to such change.

21.3   Safe Conditions. Whenever a faculty member reports a condition which the faculty member feels represents a violation of safety or health rules and regulations or which is an unreasonable hazard to persons or property, such conditions shall be promptly investigated. The appropriate administrator shall reply to the concern, in writing, if the faculty member's concern is communicated in writing.

21.4   Limitation on Personal Liability.
    (a) In the event a faculty member is sued for an act, event, or omission which may fall within the scope of Section 768.28, Florida Statutes, the faculty member should notify the President's office as soon as possible after receipt of the summons commencing the action in order that the Board may fulfill its obligation. Failure to notify the employer promptly may affect the rights of the parties.

    (b) For information purposes, the following pertinent language of Section 768.28(9), Florida Statutes, is reproduced herein.

    No officer, employee, or agent of the state or of any of its subdivisions shall be held personally liable in tort or named as a party defendant in any action for any injury or damage suffered as a result of any act, event, or omission of action in the scope of her or his employment or function, unless such officer, employee, or agent acted in bad faith or with malicious purpose or in a manner exhibiting wanton and willful disregard of human rights, safety, or property.

21.5   Travel Advances. The University will, to the extent permitted by state law and rule, provide travel advances, upon request, of up to eighty (80) percent of budgeted expenses for authorized travel of longer than five (5) consecutive days.

21.6   Working Papers Rights. Consistent with law, the provisions of Article 18, and the legitimate interests of the University, faculty members shall have the right to control of their personal correspondence, notes, raw data, and other working papers.

21.7   Protection for Whistleblowers. Faculty members are notified that Section 112.3187, Florida Statutes, provides protection to whistleblowers and delineates their rights and responsibilities.

Article 22
SABBATICAL AND PROFESSIONAL DEVELOPMENT LEAVE

22.1   Policy. Sabbatical and professional development leaves shall be made available by the Board to faculty members who meet the requirements set forth below. Such leaves are granted to increase a faculty member's value to the University through enhanced opportunities for professional development, research, writing, or other forms of creative activity.

22.2   Sabbatical Leaves.
    (a) Types of Sabbatical Leaves.
    (1) The Board shall make available to each faculty member whose application has been reviewed and approved as described below, a sabbatical leave for two (2) semesters (i.e., one (1) academic year) at half (1/2) pay.
    (2) Each year, the Board will make available at least one (1) sabbatical leave at full-pay for one (1) semester for each forty (40) eligible faculty members, subject to the conditions set forth below.

    (b) Eligibility.
    (1) Full-time tenured faculty members with at least six (6) years of full-time service shall be eligible for sabbatical leaves.
    (2) A faculty member who has taken a sabbatical leave shall not normally be eligible for another until she or he has completed six (6) more years of full-time service.

    (c) Application and Selection.
    (1) Each application shall include a statement describing the program and activities to be followed while on sabbatical, the expected increase in value of the faculty member to the University and the faculty member's academic discipline, specific results anticipated from the leave, any anticipated supplementary income, the dates of all previous sabbaticals taken, and a statement that the applicant agrees to comply with the conditions of the sabbatical leave program as described in this Article.
    (2) Sabbatical leaves shall be granted unless the University has determined that the conditions set forth in this Section have not been met or that departmental/unit staffing considerations preclude such leave from being granted. In this latter instance, the faculty member shall be provided the sabbatical leave the following year, or at a later time as agreed to by the faculty member and the University. The period of postponement shall be credited for eligibility for a subsequent sabbatical leave.
    (3) If there are more applicants for one (1) semester sabbaticals at full-pay than available

sabbaticals, a committee shall rank the applications. The committee shall be elected by and from the faculty members eligible for sabbatical leave. The chairperson shall be selected by the President or representative. The committee, in ranking the applications, shall consider the benefits of the proposed program to the faculty member, the University and the profession; an equitable distribution of sabbaticals among colleges, divisions, schools, departments, and disciplines within the University; the length of time since the faculty member was relieved of teaching duties for the purpose of research and other scholarly activities; and the length of service since previous sabbatical or initial appointment. The committee shall submit a ranked list of recommended faculty members to the President or representative. The President or representative shall make appointments from the list and consult with the committee prior to an appointment that does not follow the committee's ranking.

22.3   Professional Development Leave.

(a) Types of Professional Development Leave. Each year, the University or its representatives will make available at least one (1) professional development leave at full-pay for one (1) semester or half (1/2) pay for two (2) semesters, for each twenty (20) eligible faculty members, subject to the conditions set forth in this Article.

(b) Eligibility for Professional Development Leave.

(1) Full-time faculty members with three (3) or more years of service shall be eligible for professional development leaves, except those faculty members who are serving in tenure-earning or tenured positions.

(2) A faculty member who has taken a professional development leave shall not normally be eligible for another until she or he has completed three (3) more years of full-time service.

(c) Application and Selection.

(1) Application for professional development leave shall contain an appropriate outline of the project or work to be accomplished during the leave and a statement of length of service since the last professional development leave (or initial appointment).

(2) The Board or its representative shall approve applications when the University believes that completion of the project or work would improve the productivity of the department or function of which the faculty member is a part. Criteria for selection of professional development leave applicants shall be specified and made available to eligible faculty members.

(d) A faculty member who takes a professional development leave and fails to spend the time as stated in the application shall reimburse the University for the salary received during such leave.

22.4 Conditions Applicable to both Sabbatical and Professional Development Leaves.

(a) Eligible faculty members shall be notified annually regarding eligibility requirements and application procedures and deadlines.

(b) No more than one (1) faculty member per ten (10) in a department/unit need be awarded a sabbatical or professional development leave at the same time.

(c) A faculty member who is compensated through a contract or grant may receive a sabbatical or professional development leave only if the contract or grant allows for such leaves and the faculty member meets all other eligibility requirements.

(d) While on sabbatical or professional development leave, the faculty member's salary shall be one half (1/2) pay for two (2) semesters (one (1) academic year), or full-pay for one semester.

(e) Contributions normally made by the Board to retirement and Social Security programs shall be continued on a basis proportional to the salary received. Board contributions normally made to faculty insurance programs and any other faculty benefit programs shall be continued during the leave.

(f) Eligible faculty members shall continue to accrue annual and sick leave on a full-time basis during the leave.

(g) While on leave, a faculty member shall be permitted to receive funds for travel and living expenses, and other leave-related expenses, from sources other than the University such as fellowships, grants-in-aid, and contracts and grants, to assist in accomplishing the purposes of the leave. Receipt of funds for such purposes shall not result in reduction of the faculty member's University salary. Grants for such financial assistance from other sources may, but need not, be administered through the University. If financial assistance is received in the form of salary, the University salary shall normally be reduced by the amount necessary to bring the total income of the sabbatical period to a level comparable to not more than 125 % of the faculty member's current year salary rate. Employment unrelated to the purpose of the sabbatical leave is governed by the provisions of Article 19, Conflict of Interest and Outside Activity.

(h) The faculty member must return to University employment for at least one (1) academic year following participation in the program. Agreements to the contrary must be reduced to writing prior to participation. Return of salary received during the program shall be required in those instances where neither of the above is satisfied.

(i) The faculty member must, within sixty (60) days after the start of the next semester following the leave, provide a written report describing the faculty member's accomplishments during the leave to the president or representative, dean and department chair. This report shall include information regarding the activities undertaken during the leave, the results accomplished during the leave as they affect the faculty member and the University, and research or other scholarly work produced or expected to be produced as a result of the leave. The accrual of service credit toward future sabbaticals shall not commence until such time as the report is provided.

22.5 Other Study Leave.

(a) Job-Required. A faculty member required to take academic course work as part of assigned duties shall not be required to charge time spent attending classes during the work day to accrued leave.

(b) Job-Related. A faculty member may, at the discretion of the supervisor, be permitted to attend up to six (6) credits of course work per semester during work, provided that:

(1) The course work is directly related to the faculty member's professional responsibilities;

(2) The supervisor determines that the absence will not interfere with the proper operation of the work unit;

(3) The supervisor believes that completion of the course work would improve the productivity of the department or function of which the faculty member is a part; and

(4) The faculty member's work schedule can be adjusted to accommodate such job-related study without reduction in the total number of work hours required per pay period.

(c) Faculty members may, in accordance with this Article, use accrued annual leave for job-related study.

22.6 Retraining. The Board may, at its discretion, provide opportunities for retraining of faculty members when it is in the University's best interests. Such opportunities may be provided to faculty members who are laid off, to those who are reassigned, or in other appropriate circumstances. These retraining opportunities may include enrollment in tuition-free courses under the provisions of Article 24 and this Article.

Article 23
SALARIES

23.1 Policy.

(a) The Board and the UFF agree that salary is an important positive factor in the recruitment and retention of strong researchers and teachers, and that a salary increase can be a powerful positive incentive for meritorious performance.

(b) Merit-based salary increases and bonuses are based on the duties assigned pursuant to Article 9 and the faculty evaluation criteria and procedures established by departments/units pursuant to Article 10.

(c) The President shall, in his or her annual budget request, request the Board of Governors to seek from the Florida Legislature recurring funds to be allocated toward meritorious performance, correcting market inequities within the faculty, and raising average FSU faculty salaries to the national average for top 25 public research universities with very high research activity as reflected in the most recent Oklahoma State University survey and similar sources as appropriate. The distribution of any salary increase funds obtained by the University shall be collectively bargained by the BOT and UFF.

23.2 Categories of Salary Increases.
 (a) Increases to faculty salaries may be awarded in the following categories:
  (1) Promotion increases, pursuant to Section 23.3;
  (2) Sustained Performance Increases, pursuant to 23.4;
  (3) Merit Salary increases/bonuses, pursuant to Section 23.5;
  (4) Market equity increases, pursuant to Section 23.6;
  (5) Awards, pursuant to Section 23.7;
  (6) Legislative increases/bonuses, pursuant to Section 23.8;
  (7) Administrative discretionary increases, pursuant to Section 23.9;
  (8) Other payments, pursuant to Section 23.10.

 (b) Faculty base salaries shall only be modified as provided in this Article and for changes between 9- and 12-month appointments as provided in Article 8.5(a).

23.3 Promotion.
 (a) For fiscal year 2013-2014, promotion increases were granted pursuant to Article 14 in the amount of twelve percent (12%) added to the base salary in recognition of promotion to the ranks of Associate in ___, Associate Professor, Associate Curator, Associate Scholar/Scientist/Engineer, and Associate University Librarian and in the amount of fifteen percent (15%) added to the base salary in recognition of promotion to the ranks of Professor, Curator, Scholar/Scientist/Engineer, Research Associate or University Librarian. Promotional increases were implemented on August 8, 2013.

 (b) For fiscal year 2014-2015, promotion increases were granted pursuant to Article 14 in the amount of twelve percent (12%) added to the base salary in recognition of promotion to the ranks of Associate Professor, Associate Curator, Teaching Faculty II, Instructional Specialist II, Research Faculty II, Associate in Research, and Associate University Librarian and in the amount of fifteen percent (15%) added to the base salary in recognition of promotion to the ranks of Professor, Curator, Teaching Faculty III, Instructional Specialist III, Research Faculty III, Senior Research Associate or University Librarian. Promotional increases were implemented on August 8, 2014.

 (c) For fiscal year 2015-2016, promotion increases will be granted pursuant to Article 14 in the amount of twelve percent (12%) added to the base salary in recognition of promotion to the ranks of Associate Professor, Associate Curator, Teaching Faculty II, Instructional Specialist II, Research Faculty II, Associate in Research, and Associate University Librarian and in the amount of fifteen percent (15%) added to the base salary in recognition of promotion to the ranks of Professor, Curator, Teaching Faculty III, Instructional Specialist III, Research Faculty III, Senior Research Associate or University Librarian. Promotional increases shallhave an effective date of August 10, 2015.

Article 23
SALARIES

23.4. Sustained Performance Increases.

(a) Sustained performance increases are designed to recognize the high quality performance of eligible senior faculty who have continued to contribute substantially to the University in their assigned areas of teaching, scholarship/creative activity, and service.

(b) For fiscal year 2013-2014, full professors and eminent scholars who have been in rank for seven years and who have been rated as "Satisfactory" on their most recent sustained performance evaluation conducted in accordance with Article 10.8 received a 3% increase to base salary. Those faculty members who have received an SPI are not eligible for another SPI until they receive their next satisfactory sustained performance evaluation. Full professors who received an SPP award in fiscal year 2010-2011 are not eligible for a sustained performance increase during the 2013-2014 fiscal year. Full professors and eminent scholars who have not received a sustained performance evaluation within the past seven years must receive one, pursuant to Article 10.8, in order to be eligible for a sustained performance increase. Sustained performance increases were implemented with an effective date of August 8, 2013.

(c) Fiscal year 2014-2015

(1) Full professors and eminent scholars who have been rated above "Official Concern" on their 2014 sustained performance evaluation conducted in accordance with Article 10.8 shall receive a 3% increase to base salary. Full professors who received an SPP award in fiscal year 2010-2011 are not eligible for a sustained performance increase during the 2014-2015 fiscal year. Faculty members who have not received a sustained performance evaluation within the past seven years must receive one, pursuant to Article 10.8, in order to be eligible for a sustained performance increase. Sustained performance increases shall be implemented with an effective date of August 8, 2014.

(2) Research Faculty III, Teaching Faculty III, Senior Research Associate, Instructional Specialist III, University Librarians, and Curators who have been working at FSU for seven years or more after their promotion to top rank or equivalent and who have received above "Official Concern" rating in each of the previous seven years annual evaluations shall receive a 3% increase to base salary. Faculty members who have not received a performance evaluation for the most recent of the past seven years must receive one in order to be eligible for a sustained performance increase. Sustained performance increases shall be implemented with an effective date of August 8, 2014.

(d) Fiscal year 2015-2016

(1) Full professors and eminent scholars who have been working at FSU for seven years after their promotion to top rank and who have been rated above "Official Concern" on their most recent sustained performance evaluation conducted in accordance with Article 10.8 shall receive a 3% increase to base salary. Faculty members who have not received a sustained performance evaluation within the past seven years must receive one, pursuant to Article 10.8, in order to be eligible for a sustained performance increase. Sustained performance increases shall be implemented with an effective date of August 10, 2015.

(2) Research Faculty III, Teaching Faculty III, Senior Research Associate, Instructional Specialist III, University Librarians, and Curators who have been working at FSU for seven years after their promotion to top rank and who have received above "Official Concern" rating in each of the previous seven years' annual evaluations shall receive a 3% increase to base salary. Faculty members who have not received a performance evaluation for the most recent of the past seven years must receive one in order to be eligible for a sustained performance increase. Sustained performance increases shall be implemented with an effective date of August 10, 2015.

23.5   Merit Salary Increases / Bonuses. For fiscal year 2013-2014, the amount allocated for recurring merit salary increases was 1.7% distributed as outlined below. For fiscal year 2014-2015, the amount allocated for recurring merit salary increases was1.75% distributed as outlined below.
   (a) Eligibility.
      (1) Nine-month faculty members must have been employed by the University in a salaried position on or before August 8, 2014 and be in active payroll status on the effective date of the increase, in order to be eligible.
      (2) Twelve-month faculty members must have been employed by the University on or before August 8, 2014 and be in active payroll status on the effective date of the increase, in order to be eligible.

   (b) Performance Increases.
      (1) For fiscal year 2013-2014, in recognition of their high level of performance, eligible faculty members received a recurring 1.1% performance-based pay increase. These increases were implemented on October 1, 2013. These amounts were prorated for part-time faculty members. Faculty members must have received an overall annual evaluation of "satisfactory" for calendar year 2012 performance in order to be eligible.
      (2) For fiscal year 2014-2015, in recognition of their high level of performance, eligible faculty members received a recurring $1500 performance-based pay increase. These increases were implemented on September 26, 2014. These amounts were prorated for part-time faculty members. Faculty members must have received an overall annual evaluation of at least "meets FSU's high expectations" for calendar year 2013 performance in order to be eligible.
      (3) For fiscal year 2015-2016, in recognition of their high level of performance, eligible faculty members will receive a recurring one-half percent (0.5%) performance-based pay increase added to the base salary as of May 7, 2015. These amounts shall be prorated for part-time faculty members. Faculty members must have received an overall annual evaluation of at least "meets FSU's high expectations" for calendar year 2014 performance in order to be eligible. These increases shall be effective August 28, 2015, provided that the agreement is ratified no later than August 10, 2015. If the agreement is ratified at a later date, the increases shall be effective one to two (1 to 2) pay periods after the ratification date.
      (4) For fiscal year 2015-2016, in recognition of their high level of performance, eligible specialized faculty members shall receive an additional recurring one percent (1%) performance-

based pay increase for a cumulative total of one and a half percent (1.5%) added to the base salary as of May 7, 2015. These amounts shall be prorated for part-time faculty members. Specialized faculty members must have received an overall annual evaluation of at least "meets FSU's high expectations" for calendar year 2014 performance in order to be eligible. These increases shall be effective August 28, 2015, provided that the agreement is ratified no later than August 10, 2015. If the agreement is ratified at a later date, the increases shall be effective one to two (1 to 2) pay periods after the ratification date.

(c) Performance Bonuses.

(1) For fiscal year 2014-2015, eligible faculty members received a one-time performance bonus. These bonuses were reflected in the faculty member's December 12, 2014 paycheck. These amounts were prorated for part-time faculty members.

(2) The amount of the performance bonuses was determined by calculating the difference in E&G funded salaries between the dates of August 8, 2014, and the effective date of the Performance Increases outlined in Section 23.5(b), and were equally distributed in lump sum bonuses among eligible faculty members, regardless of funding source.

(d) Departmental Merit.

(1) For fiscal year 2013-2014, the amount allocated for recurring departmental merit increases was a total of one-half of one percent (0.5%) of the in-unit salary base, to be distributed based on the Spring 2013 Annual Merit Evaluation and in compliance with the provisions below. Departmental merit increases were implemented on October 25, 2013.

a. The distribution of departmental merit was made in accordance with the Department/Unit Faculty Evaluation Criteria and Procedures developed pursuant to Article 10.4 (Merit Evaluations).

b. All department plans and lists were subject to approval by the appropriate dean and the provost, who had the authority to reject plans that do not comply with Article 10.4.

(2) For fiscal year 2014-2015, the amount allocated for recurring departmental merit increases was a total of one and fifty-five hundredths percent (1.55%) of the in-unit salary base, to be distributed based on the Spring 2014 department/unit Annual Merit Evaluation and in compliance with the provisions below. Departmental merit increases were implemented on November 7, 2014.

(3) For fiscal year 2015-2016, the amount allocated for recurring departmental merit increases shall be a total of one and seventy-five hundredths percent (1.75%) of the in-unit salary base as of May 7, 2015, to be distributed based on the Spring 2015 department/unit Annual Merit Evaluation and in compliance with the provisions below. Departmental merit increases shall be effective October 9, 2015, provided that the agreement is ratified by August 10, 2015. If the agreement is ratified at a later date, the increases shall be effective five to six (5-6) pay periods after the ratification date.

a. Eligibility.

i. Nine-month faculty members must be employed by the University in a salaried position on or before August 9, 2014 and be in active payroll status on the effective date of the increase in order to be eligible.

ii. Twelve-month faculty members must be employed by the University on or before August 8, 2014, and be in active payroll status on the effective date of the increase in order to be eligible.

iii. The determination regarding eligibility for departmental merit shall be made in accordance with the Department/Unit Faculty Evaluation Criteria and Procedures developed pursuant to Article 10.4 (Merit Evaluations).

b. All department plans and lists are subject to approval by the appropriate dean and the provost, who have the authority to reject plans that do not comply with Article 10.4.

c. The distribution of departmental merit shall be made in accordance with the Department/Unit Faculty Evaluation Criteria and Procedures developed pursuant to Article 10.4 (Merit Evaluations).

(e) Deans' Merit.

(1) For fiscal year 2013-2014, the amount allocated for recurring deans' merit increases was a total of 0.1% of the in-unit salary base and was implemented on October 25, 2013.

a. The deans distributed these increases to in-unit faculty members to recognize meritorious performance (including differential departmental performance) to department chairs, faculty members who report directly to deans, and other faculty members.

(2) For fiscal year 2014-2015, the amount allocated for recurring deans' merit increases was a total of 0.2% of the in-unit salary base and was implemented on November 7, 2014.

a. The deans shall distribute these increases to in-unit faculty members to recognize meritorious performance (including differential departmental performance) to department chairs, faculty members who report directly to deans, and other faculty members.

(3) For fiscal year 2015-2016, the amount allocated for recurring dean's merit increases shall be a total of thirty-five hundredths percent (0.35%) of the in-unit salary base as of May 7, 2015, and shall be effective October 9, 2015, provided that the agreement is ratified by August 10, 2015. If the agreement is ratified at a later date, the increases shall be effective five to six (5 to 6) pay periods after the ratification date.

(e) Deans' Merit Bonus. For fiscal year 2013-2014, non-recurring merit bonuses were awarded proportionately in each department/unit in the amount of $600 to 35% of in-unit faculty in each department/unit in June 2014. The determination of the recipients was made by deans/directors, and took into account department/unit merit ratings from Spring 2013.

23.6. Market Equity. The UFF and the University acknowledge and agree that recruiting and maintaining a top-quality faculty requires market equity with peer institutions. The University and the UFF shall periodically assess market equity in relation to faculty salaries at aspirational peer institutions, which are among the top 25 public US universities, members of the American Association of Universities, and "Very High Research Universities" category in the Oklahoma

Article 23
SALARIES

State University annual Faculty Salary Survey (OSU Salary Survey). Market equity shall be based on position, rank, discipline, experience, and performance.

(a) Eligibility. For purposes of Section 23.6, for fiscal year 2015-2016, "eligible faculty members" shall include in-unit Eminent Scholars, Full Professors, Associate Professors, and Assistant Professors. A faculty member in a visiting position is not eligible for the Market Equity increase.

(1) Nine-month faculty members must have been employed by the University in a salaried position as of August 8, 2014, and be in active payroll status on the effective date of the increase, in order to be eligible. Twelve-month faculty members must have been employed by the University in a salaried position as of August 8, 2014, and be in active payroll status on the effective date of the increase, in order to be eligible.

(2) Any faculty member who has received (1) an overall rating of "Unsatisfactory," "Inadequate," or "Does Not Meet FSU's High Expectations" on any annual evaluation in the last 7 years, or (2) more than one overall rating of "Official Concern" in the last 7 years, will be ineligible for a Market Equity increase. Additionally, any faculty member who has received a notice of contract non-renewal will be ineligible for a Market Equity increase.

(b) CIP Code Determination. The Provost, in consultation with the Office of Faculty Development and Advancement, shall assign each eligible faculty member a "Classification of Instructional Program 2010" (CIP) code reflecting her/his major discipline as of December 1, 2014. CIP codes are maintained by the National Center for Education Statistics. (http://nces.ed.gov/ipeds/cipcode/).

(1) The CIP code must correspond to a degree program offered by the University. Eligible faculty members shall be assigned a CIP code corresponding to a degree program offered by the faculty member's "Tenure Home" department. For interdisciplinary faculty members, the CIP code most closely reflecting the majority of their effort shall be used.

(2) The assignment of the CIP code shall not be subject to grievance under this Agreement, but shall be reviewable under the procedures set forth in Section 23.6(i).

(c) Total Salary. The "total salary" for eligible faculty members shall include the annual salary, excluding summer salary for nine-month faculty members, measured as of December 1, 2014, plus any payments from Direct Support Organizations made during the 2014-2015 academic year, plus the salary earned from overload appointments during the 2014-2015 academic year when that faculty member has received the appointment consistently for three (3) academic years.

(d) Nine-Month Equivalent Salary. The "nine-month equivalent salary" for eligible nine-month faculty members is the total salary as defined in Section 23.6(c). For eligible twelve-month faculty members, the nine-month equivalent salary is the total salary as defined in Section 23.6(c), multiplied by 0.818 (9/11).

(e) Base Equity Salary. A "base equity salary" shall be established for each eligible faculty member, which shall be the nine-month mean salary for the corresponding rank and CIP code from the annual OSU Salary Survey for "Very High Research Universities," prorated by FTE. For purposes hereunder, the rank of Eminent Scholar shall be combined with the rank of Full Professor.

(f) Target Equity Salary. A "target equity salary" shall be established for each eligible faculty member. This figure shall be the base equity salary determined from Section 23.6(e), adjusted for the following:

(1) A years-in-rank adjustment shall be made, which shall be plus or minus, as appropriate, one percent (1.0%) of the base equity salary multiplied by the difference between the faculty member's number of years in their current rank at FSU and the average years in that rank at FSU for all eligible faculty members under this section. The average years in rank for eligible Associate Professors shall be 4 years. Eligible Associate Professors shall not receive credit in the form of a years-in-rank adjustment for their time in rank at FSU over 8 years.

(2) In addition, for eligible faculty members who have received any departmental or deans' merit increase from August 9, 2005 through December 31, 2014, the total amount of such merit increases shall be added to the faculty member's target equity salary.

(g) Equity Salary Difference. The "equity salary difference" for each eligible faculty member is the difference between the faculty member's target equity salary as defined in section 23.6(f) and their nine-month equivalent salary as defined in section 23.6(d). If this figure is less than zero, the equity salary difference is defined as zero.

(1) For eligible twelve-month faculty members, this value is multiplied by 1.222 (or 11/9).

(h) Distribution.

(1) For fiscal year 2015-2016, the total E&G funds available for Market Equity purposes shall be $2.0 million ($2,000,000).

(2) The Needed Market Equity for the University is defined herein as the sum of the "equity salary differences," as defined in Section 23.6(g), for all eligible E&G-funded faculty.

(3) The Available Market Equity Ratio is defined herein as the total funds available for Market Equity purposes, as described in Section 23.6(h)(1), divided by the Needed Market Equity for the University.

(4) The Market Equity Increase for an eligible faculty member shall be equal to the Available Market Equity Ratio multiplied by the faculty member's equity salary difference.

(5) The maximum increase for an eligible faculty member shall be $10,000. The remaining funds available after the cap is applied shall be distributed to the remaining eligible faculty members by multiplying the Available Market Equity Ratio by the remaining faculty member's "equity salary difference."

(6) The increases shall be effective September 25, 2015, provided that the agreement is ratified by August 10, 2015. If the agreement is ratified at a later date, the increases shall be

effective four to five (4 to 5) pay periods after the ratification date.

(i)   CIP Code Assignment Review Procedure. An eligible faculty member may request a review of her or his CIP code determination by submitting a written request to the Vice President for Faculty Development and Advancement. The request shall contain a general description of the determination in question and copies of relevant documentation. Upon receipt of a request, the determination shall be reviewed by a joint committee composed of three members selected by the Vice President for Faculty Development and Advancement and three faculty representatives selected by the UFF-FSU. Within 15 days of receiving the request, the committee shall review the request, make a decision regarding the determination, and notify the faculty member. In the event that the committee vote results in a tie, a mutually agreed upon chairperson will be selected by the committee and shall make the final determination. The decision of the committee shall be final and binding. 23.7.   Awards.

(a) The Board may provide stipends in supplement of base salary and one-time bonuses for the following awards:

(1) University or college Teaching Awards;
(2) University Advising Awards;
(3) Robert O. Lawton Distinguished Professor;
(4) Developing Scholar Awards;
(5) Distinguished Research Professor;
(6) Graduate Faculty Mentor Awards;
(7) Superior Liberal Studies Honors Teaching Awards;
(8) Foundation Awards for Faculty Recognition;
(9) Distinguished University Scholar Awards;
(10)   Honors Thesis Mentor Awards;
(11)   Post-doc Faculty Mentor Awards;
(12)   Compensation may be provided with newly established awards, subject to collective bargaining.

(b) At the end of each academic year, the Board shall provide the UFF with a complete list, in a mutually agreeable electronic format, of all awards made under this section during the previous twelve (12) month period. For each such increase, the list shall provide the name and classification/rank of the individual receiving the award, the nature of the award (stipend or one-time bonus), the name of the award, and the amount of the award.

(c) Each year, at the same time as the Board provides the list described in (b) above, the Board shall provide the UFF with copies of the selection criteria and procedures for all awards named in said list.

23.8 Legislative Increases/Bonuses.

(a) Competitive pay adjustments fiscal year 2013-2014. Legislation providing for recurring increases of $1000 for faculty members paid more than $40,000 annual salary rate as of

September 30, 2013 and recurring increases of $1400 for faculty members paid $40,000 or less annual salary rate as of September 30, 2013 were implemented on October 1, 2013. The amounts were prorated for part-time faculty members.

(b) Merit Bonuses for Fiscal year 2013-2014 were distributed in accordance with 23.5(e) Deans' Merit Bonus.

(c) If the Legislature appropriates any funds for salary increases or bonuses, the disposition of those funds shall be subject to negotiation between the BOT and the UFF.

23.9 Administrative Discretionary Increases.

(a) For fiscal years 2013-2014 and 2014-2015, the University provided salary increases beyond the increases specified above under this section not to exceed one percent (1%) of the total salary rate of faculty members who are in an employment relationship with the University on the first day of May immediately preceding the beginning of the fiscal year for the circumstances listed in 23.9. For fiscal years 2015-2016, the University may provide salary increases beyond the increases specified above under this section not to exceed one percent (1%) of the total salary rate of faculty members who are in an employment relationship with the University on the first day of May immediately preceding the beginning of the fiscal year for the circumstances listed in 23 9:

(1) Counter-offers made in response to verified written offers from comparable or aspirational educational and research institutions.

(2) Endowed/named chairs at the time they are awarded.

(3) Extraordinary accomplishments recognized by the national or international academic or professional community or recognition internal to the University, that are substantially beyond the minimum performance criteria for the top departmental merit category as approved by the faculty according to Article 10.

(4) Equity adjustments to correct salary inversions and compression relative to rank and history of annual performance evaluations. For tenured or tenure-earning faculty members equity adjustments shall follow the principles set forth in the Market Equity and FSU Faculty Salaries Report of the Joint Study Group, dated January 24, 2007, and, for all faculty members, will be based on written criteria and procedures published by the dean of each college/unit and provided to the UFF Chapter at least 45 days before implementation.

(5) Increased duties and responsibilities. A salary increase may be awarded to a faculty member for a substantial increase in duties or responsibilities, such as service as a department chair or an analogous responsibility.

(6) Recognition for Distinguished Faculty. This category is designated to recognize exceptional performance of faculty members. The University may provide salary increases to faculty members for extraordinary performance. For faculty members in tenured or tenure-seeking positions, the University may assign the title of "Assistant/Associate Professor with Distinction" or "Distinguished Professor" to the recipients of these increases. For faculty members in "Specialized Faculty" positions, the University may assign the words "With

Distinction" after the title that the faculty member currently holds.

(7) Notice shall be given of any discretionary increases that are approved by the administration but fall outside of the categories listed above or are to be effective after June 30, 2016. The UFF will have 15 days from the date of receipt to object to the increase. If an objection is made, the increase shall not be implemented.

(b) Within thirty (30) days after the effective date, or as soon as practicable, the University shall provide to the UFF a written notification of each Administrative Discretionary Increase. The notification shall state the name of the faculty member, the rank and discipline of the faculty member, the amount of the increase and the reason for the increase. The report shall include the following supporting evidence:

(1) For counter-offers, a copy of the verified written offer.

(2) For endowed/named chairs, a copy of the criteria and procedures for the award of the chair.

(3) For extraordinary accomplishments, an explanation of how the accomplishments exceed the minimum criteria for the top merit category of the department/unit; or in instances where the extraordinary accomplishment is an external award or similar, the specific external award or alternative criteria which is considered "prestigious" or "highly prestigious."

(4) For equity adjustments, the salaries and history of annual accomplishments of the group(s) relative to which the inequity is to be corrected.

(5) For increased duties and responsibilities, the signed annual Assignments of Responsibilities for the year preceding the change and the new one reflecting the increased duties and responsibilities.

(6) For recognition of distinction, the specific external award or alternative criteria which justifies the designation of "Distinguished" or "with Distinction."

(c) Any court-ordered or court-approved salary increase or any salary increase to settle a legitimate broad-based employment dispute shall not be subject to the terms and limitations of this section.

(d) With the exception of section 23.9(a)(7), the discretion to grant all other salary increases authorized by this section shall cease on June 30, 2016, and shall not survive such expiration as part of the status quo.

(e) All documents provided to the UFF under section 23.9 shall be in electronic format and delivered to two representatives designated by the UFF.

23.10 Other Payments. Not applicable.

23.11 Report to Faculty Members. All faculty members shall receive notice of their salary increase on the Appendix G form or by an amended employment contract within two weeks of the effective date or as soon thereafter as practicable. Faculty members may review their pay histories by accessing the myFSU portal, opening the "Human Resources" link, and then opening the "Compensation History" link.

23.12   Report to the UFF.

(a) No later than fifteen (15) days after a pay period in which a salary increase (including increases to base rate, awards, and bonuses) is reflected, the Board shall report to the UFF in a mutually agreed electronic format a list of all faculty salary increases reflected in that pay period.

(b) The report shall be formatted in easily readable columns and shall include:
(1) the name of each faculty member;
(2) the name of the department/unit;
(3) the rank of the faculty member;
(4) the date of promotion or appointment of the faculty member to the rank;
(5) the faculty member's previous year's salary rate;
(6) the amount received in each salary increase category during the previous twelve months, according to categorization of salary increases identified in this agreement;
(7) the faculty member's new salary rate.

(c) A printed copy of each department's portion of the report shall be placed on file in the department, available upon request to any faculty member of the department, as well as in the main library, along with the documents prescribed in Article 7.

23.13 Contract and Grant-Funded Increases.

(a) Faculty members on contracts or grants shall receive salary increases equivalent to similar faculty members on regular funding, provided that such salary increases are permitted by the terms of the contract or grant and adequate funds are available for this purpose in the contract or grant.

(b) Nothing contained herein shall prevent faculty members whose salaries are funded by grant agencies from being allotted raises higher than those provided to other faculty members under this Agreement, subject to the approval of the University President or designee. For example, market equity adjustments pursuant to 23.9(a)(4) may be awarded to employees funded by grants.

23.14 Grievability. Unless provided for otherwise in this Article, the only issues to be addressed in a grievance filed pursuant to Article 20 alleging violation of this Article are whether there is unlawful discrimination under Article 6, or whether there is incorrect application of the provisions of one or more sections of this Article. No grievance may be brought disputing an administrator's or an advisory committee's evaluative judgment of a faculty member's merit.

23.15   Upon request the BOT will offer assistance to faculty members who wish to reserve salary dollars earned for time periods when they do not have an appointment with the university by providing the appropriate calculation for deductions to the faculty member as well as guidance on establishing personal direct deposits via the payroll system.

23.16   Any waiver of some or all of the right to bargain over the salaries or other compensation of bargaining unit employees contained in this Article, excluding administrative discretionary increases pursuant to Section 23.9(a)(7), shall expire on June 30, 2016.

Article 24
BENEFITS

24.1   Benefits and Benefit Improvements.
    (a) Benefits are an important tool for attracting and retaining top quality faculty members. The Board and UFF strive to offer competitive benefits.

    (b) The Board and the UFF support legislation to provide adequate and affordable health insurance to all faculty members.

24.2   Part-Time Faculty Members. Part-time faculty members, except those in positions funded from Other Personal Services funds, are entitled to employer-funded benefits under the provisions of state law and the rules of the Department of Management Services. Part-time faculty members should contact the Human Resources office to determine the nature and extent of the benefits for which they are eligible.

24.3   Retirement Credit. Retirement credit for faculty members who are authorized to take uncompensated or partially compensated leaves of absence shall be granted in accordance with state law and the rules of the Division of Retirement as they may exist at the time leave is granted. The current Florida Retirement System rules also require that to receive full retirement credit, the faculty member on uncompensated or partially compensated leave must make payment of the retirement contribution that would otherwise be made by the University, plus interest, if applicable. Faculty members who are to take such a leave of absence should contact the Human Resources office for complete information prior to taking the leave.

24.4   Benefits for Retired Faculty Members.
    (a) Faculty members retired from the University shall be eligible, upon request, and on the same basis as other faculty members, subject to University policies, to receive the following benefits at the University:
        (1) FSU identification card;
        (2) Use of the University library (i.e., public rooms, lending and research service);
        (3) Listing in the University directory;
        (4) Placement on designated University mailing lists;
        (5) A University parking decal;
        (6) Use of University recreational facilities (retired faculty members may be charged fees different from those charged to other employees for the use of such facilities);

(7) The right to enroll in courses without payment of fees, on a space available basis, in accordance with the provisions of Section 1009.26(4), Florida Statutes;

(8) A mailbox in the department/unit from which the faculty member retired, subject to space availability; and

(9) A University e-mail address and Internet access.

(b) In accordance with University policy, and on a space available basis, the University is encouraged to grant a retired faculty member's request for office or laboratory space.

(c) With the exception of retirees who participated in the Optional Retirement Program, retired faculty members of any state-administered retirement system are entitled to health insurance subsidy payments in accordance with Section 112.363, Florida Statutes.

24.5 Public Employee Retirement Programs.

The Board and the UFF support legislation to provide comprehensive retirement programs for all faculty members. Faculty members have the option of electing Florida Retirement System (FRS) Pension Plan, Investment Plan, or choosing the Optional Retirement Plan (ORP). The Deferred Retirement Option Program (DROP) is a retirement program within the FRS Pension Plan that allows a faculty member to retire and have FRS benefits accumulate in the FRS Trust Fund earning interest while the faculty member continues to work for up to five years. Newly hired faculty members will receive retirement plan enrollment information from the Human Resources department upon being hired at the University.

24.6 Optional Retirement Program.

(a) An Optional Retirement Program is provided for faculty members who are employed for no less than one academic year including the following provisions:

(1) Faculty members who are in the collective bargaining unit and otherwise eligible for membership in the Florida Retirement System.

(2) Any faculty member whose Optional Retirement Program eligibility results from initial employment will be enrolled as a member of the Optional Retirement Program. If the faculty member does not execute an annuity contract with an Optional Retirement Program approved provider and notify the Division of Retirement in writing within 90 days, the faculty member will be enrolled as a member of the Florida Retirement System.

(3) No accrued service credit or vested retirement benefits will be lost if a faculty member participates in the Optional Retirement Program;

(4) Benefits under the Optional Retirement Program shall be fully and immediately vested in the participating faculty members;

(5) The employer shall contribute to the Optional Retirement Program, on behalf of each faculty member participating in the program, an amount equal to the normal cost portion of the employer's contribution to the Florida Retirement System, as well as an amount equal to the employer's contribution to the Retiree Health Insurance Subsidy program on behalf of non-Optional Retirement participants (see Section 112.363(8), Florida Statutes), less a reasonable and

necessary amount, as determined by the Legislature, which shall be provided to the Division of Retirement for administering the program; and

(6) A participating faculty member may contribute to the Optional Retirement Program, by salary reduction or deduction, a percentage amount of the faculty member's gross compensation not to exceed the percentage amount contributed by the employer to the Optional Retirement Program, but in no case may such contribution exceed federal limitations.

(b) The parties agree to inform eligible faculty members regarding the existence and impact of the Optional Retirement Program upon their retirement benefits.

(c) If the UFF is concerned with the performance of any aspect of the Optional Retirement Program, whether administered by the Board or another state agency, the UFF has a right to consult with the Board regarding such concern. As a result of such consultation, the parties may agree to an approach to address the concern if it lies outside the Board's statutory authority.

24.7 Phased Retirement Program.
(a) Eligibility.
(1) Faculty members who have accrued at least six (6) years of creditable service in the Florida or Teachers Retirement System (FRS, TRS) or Optional Retirement Program (ORP), except those faculty members referenced in 24.7(a)(2), are eligible to participate in the Phased Retirement Program (PRP). Such eligibility shall expire on the faculty member's 63rd birthday. Faculty members who decide to participate must provide written notice to the University of such decision prior to the expiration of their eligibility, or thereafter forfeit such eligibility. Faculty members who choose to participate must retire with an effective date not later than 180 days, nor less than ninety (90) days, after they submit such written notice, except that when the end of this 180 day period falls within a semester, the period may be extended to no later than the beginning of the subsequent term (semester or summer, as appropriate).

(2) Faculty members not eligible to participate in the Phased Retirement Program include those who have received notice of non-reappointment, layoff, or termination, and those who participate in the State's Deferred Retirement Option Program (DROP).

(b) Program Provisions.
(1) All participants must retire and thereby relinquish all rights to tenure as described in Article 15, except as stated otherwise in this Article. Participants' retirement benefits shall be determined as provided under Florida Statutes and the rules of the Division of Retirement.

(2) Payment for Unused Leave. Participants shall, upon retirement, receive payment for any unused annual leave and sick leave to which they are entitled.

(3) Re-employment.
a. Prior to re-employment, participants in the Phased Retirement Program must remain off the University payroll for six (6) calendar months following the effective date of retirement in order to validate their retirement, as required by the Florida Division of Retirement. Participants must comply with the re-employment limitations that apply to the seventh through

twelfth month of retirement, pursuant to the provisions of either the Florida Retirement System (which includes ORP) or the Teachers Retirement System, as appropriate.

b. Participants shall be offered re-employment, in writing, by the University under an Other Personal Services (OPS) contract (NOTE: exceptions to this provision are described in Section 24.7(b)(13)) for one-half of the academic year, however, the University and faculty member may agree to less than one-half of the academic year. The written re-employment offer shall contain the text of Section 24. 7(b)(3)d below.

c. Compensation during the period of re-employment shall be at a salary proportional to the participant's salary prior to retirement, including an amount comparable to the pre-retirement employer contribution for health and life insurance and an allowance for any taxes associated with this amount. The assignment shall be scheduled within one (1) semester unless the participant and the University agree otherwise, beginning with the academic year next following the date of retirement and subject to the condition outlined in 24.7(b)(3)a.

d. Participants shall notify the University in writing regarding acceptance or rejection of an offer of re-employment not later than thirty (30) days after the faculty member's receipt of the written re-employment offer. Failure to notify the University regarding re-employment may result in the faculty member's forfeiting re-employment for that academic year.

(4) Leave for Illness/Injury.

a. Each participant shall be credited with five (5) days of leave with pay at the beginning of each full-time semester appointment. For less than full-time appointments, the leave shall be credited on a pro-rata basis with the assigned FTE. This leave is to be used in increments of not less than four (4) hours (1/2 day) when the participant is unable to perform assigned duties as a result of illness or injury of the participant or a member of the participant's immediate family. For the purposes of this Section, immediate family shall include the participant's spouse, mother, father, brother, sister, natural, adopted, or step child, or other relative living in the participant's household.

b. Such leave may be accumulated; however, upon termination of the post-retirement re-employment period, the participant shall not be reimbursed for unused leave.

(5) Personal Non-Medical Leave.

a. Each participant who was on a twelve (12) month appointment upon entering the Phased Retirement Program and whose assignment during the period of re-employment is the same as that during the twelve (12) month appointment shall be credited with five (5) days of leave with pay at the beginning of each full-time semester appointment. This leave is to be used in increments of not less than four (4) hours (1/2 day) for personal reasons unrelated to illness or injury. Except in the case of emergency, the faculty member shall provide at least two (2) days notice of the intended leave. Approval of the dates on which the faculty member wishes to take such leave shall be at the discretion of the supervisor and shall be subject to the consideration of departmental and organizational scheduling.

b. Such leave shall not be accumulated, nor shall the participant be reimbursed for unused leave upon termination of the post-retirement period.

(6) Re-employment Period.

a. The period of re-employment obligation shall extend over five (5) consecutive academic years, beginning with the academic year next following the date of retirement. No further notice of cessation of employment is required.

b. The period of re-employment obligation shall not be shortened by the University, except under the provisions of Article 16 of the Agreement. During the period of re-employment, participants are to be treated, based on status at point of retirement, as tenured faculty members or non-tenure-earning faculty members with five (5) or more years of continuous service, as appropriate, for purposes of Sections 13.2(a) and (b) of the Agreement.

(7) Declining Re-employment. A participant may decline an offer of reemployment during any academic year. Such a decision shall not extend the period of re-employment beyond the period described in Section 24.7(b)(6). At the conclusion of the re-employment period, the University may, at its option, continue to re-employ participants in this program on a year-to-year basis.

(8) Salary Increases. Participants shall receive all increases guaranteed to faculty members in established positions, in an amount proportional to their part-time appointment, and shall be eligible for non-guaranteed salary increases on the same basis as other faculty members.

(9) Preservation of Rights. Participants shall retain all rights, privileges, and benefits of employment, as provided in laws, rules, this Agreement, and University policies, subject to the conditions contained in this Article.

(10) Payroll Deductions. The UFF payroll deductions, as specified in Article 25, if applicable, shall be continued for a program participant during each reemployment period.

(11) Contracts and Grants. Nothing shall prevent the employer or the participant, consistent with law and rule, from supplementing the participant's employment with contracts or grants.

(12) The decision to participate in the Phased Retirement Program is irrevocable after the required approval document has been executed by all parties.

(13) OPS Exception. The provisions for re-employment on an OPS contract are in effect only for new PRP participants whose initial re-employment occurs during the 1992-93 academic year or thereafter.

(c) PRP Information Document. The parties agree to jointly develop written information describing the current provisions of the Phased Retirement Program in the Agreement. The University shall distribute this written information to faculty members and the UFF Chapter, upon request.

24.8 Free University Courses for Faculty Members. Full-time faculty members, including faculty members on sabbaticals or on professional development or grants-in-aid leave, may enroll for up to six (6) credit hours of instruction per term (Fall, Spring, or Summer) without payment of tuition and fees on a space available basis.

24.9   Employee Assistance Program. The Board encourages the University to expand its existing Employee Assistance Program (EAP), to include assessment, referral, follow-up consultation, short-term counseling, and other services for employees with personal, family, job stress, or substance abuse problems. Any policies created or revised by the University in the development or operation of its EAP shall be discussed in consultation with the local UFF Chapter.

24.10   Pre-tax Benefits Program. The Board shall continue to provide a pre-tax benefits program for salaried faculty members which includes the opportunity to: (1) pay for their state insurance premiums on a pre-tax basis and, (2) utilize flexible spending accounts for medical and dependent care expenses.

24.11   Bereavement Leave.
    (a) In the event of a death in the immediate family of a faculty member, the faculty member is entitled to two (2) days paid bereavement leave to attend to necessary arrangements and appropriate observances

    (b) Nothing in Section 24.11 is intended to preclude faculty members from exercising additional leave rights provided elsewhere in this agreement, including the use of unpaid leave, in association with bereavement.

Article 25
PAYROLL DEDUCTION

25.1   Deductions. The Board shall deduct, biweekly and without unauthorized interruption (provided the faculty member has funds available), the following from the pay of those faculty members in the bargaining unit who individually and voluntarily make such requests on a written authorization form such as that contained in Appendix "B" to this Agreement:
    (a) The Board shall provide one post-tax deduction code for UFF membership dues and another post-tax deduction code for PAC contributions in the amount provided by the UFF and certified in writing by the UFF state President to the Board; and

    (b) One pre-tax deduction code and one post-tax deduction code for UFF voluntary economic services programs. Deductions shall be made on a pre-tax or post-tax basis at the UFF's designation, provided there is no legal impediment to doing so and that a pre-tax deduction is permitted by the federal tax code. All such programs and deductions shall meet the requirements of state and federal law as well as Board rules and regulations. The Board shall not be obligated to adopt a UFF sponsored benefit program as an FSU sponsored benefit program. The Board and the UFF agree that any proposed change in Board rules and regulations impacting these programs and deductions shall be subject to negotiations before its implementation.

25.2   Timing of Deductions

Article 25
PAYROLL DEDUCTION

(a) The Board shall make deductions biweekly and without unauthorized interruption (provided the faculty member has funds available), beginning with the first full pay period commencing not later than seven (7) days following receipt of authorization.

(b) The UFF shall give written notice to the Board of any changes in its dues at least forty-five (45) days prior to the effective date of any such changes.

25.3 Remittance.
(a) The Board shall remit dues and other authorized deductions to the UFF State Office on a biweekly basis within thirty (30) days following the end of the pay period.

(b) Accompanying each remittance shall be a list containing the following information for each faculty member from whose salary the Board has made such deductions:
　　(1) Name and department of the faculty member;
　　(2) Biweekly salary of faculty member; and
　　(3) Amounts deducted from the faculty member's salary.

(c) The Board shall provide this list in electronic form.

25.4　Termination of Deductions.
(a) The Board's responsibility for deducting dues and other authorized deductions from a faculty member's salary shall terminate automatically upon either
　　(1) thirty (30) days written notice from the faculty member to the Board and the UFF revoking that faculty member's prior deduction authorization, or
　　(2) the transfer of the authorizing faculty member out of the bargaining unit.

(b) Consistent with the provisions of Section 1.2, the Board or representative shall notify the local UFF Chapter when it proposes to reclassify a faculty member to a classification that is not contained in the General Faculty bargaining unit.

25.5　Reinstatement of Deductions. The Board or representative shall reinstate dues deductions for faculty members who have previously filed authorization for dues deduction and are subsequently placed in leave without pay status, or who participate in the Phased Retirement Program, upon commencement of full- or part-time employment at the University.

25.6　Indemnification. The UFF assumes responsibility for (1) all claims against the Board, including the cost of defending such actions, arising from the Board's compliance with this Article, and for (2) all monies deducted under this Article and remitted to the UFF. The UFF shall promptly refund to the Board excess monies received under this Article.

25.7　Exceptions. The Board will not deduct any fines, penalties, or special assessments from the pay of any faculty member, nor is the Board obligated to provide more than four (4) payroll deduction fields for the purpose of making the deductions described in this Article.

25.8   Termination of Agreement. The Board's responsibilities under this Article shall terminate automatically upon (1) decertification of the UFF or the suspension or revocation of its certification by the Florida Public Employees Relations Commission, or (2) revocation of the UFF's deduction privilege by the Florida Public Employees Relations Commission.

Article 26
SHARED GOVERNANCE

26.1   Shared governance and academic freedom are inextricably connected. The Board and the UFF recognize the necessity of a strong system of shared governance involving faculty members in areas of academic concern and that elected bodies are the primary vehicle for such shared governance.

26.2   Elected faculty representatives shall serve on the committees that formulate and implement academic policies, or other policies that affect the terms and conditions of faculty employment.

26.3   The Board and the University Administration shall notify faculty members of any impending action affecting the faculty members and provide faculty and their departments/units sufficient opportunity to give the Board and the University Administration advice and counsel prior to the debate and final action on such matters.

26.4   Faculty members shall be included in the process of recruitment, hiring, and selection or reappointment of those administrators with supervisory responsibility over faculty.

26.5   Departments or other traditional governance structures shall have an active and significant role in academic matters. The faculties of the colleges and departments shall have the right to make their own constitutions and bylaws, by which to conduct their respective governance responsibilities. Such bylaws shall be subject to review and approval by appropriate Administration officials.

(a) The faculty members of each department/unit, by majority vote, shall establish bylaws, which must pass Administrative review. Governance in the departments/units shall be conducted in accordance with their respective bylaws, which shall be filed with the appropriate academic administrators and posted on the department/unit web sites.

(b) The bylaws of each department/unit shall include procedures for faculty members to share significantly in governance responsibilities, including recruitment of new faculty and other professionals; development of high quality programs; program review; department/unit review; department/unit reorganization; development of criteria for tenure, promotion, and merit salary increases; selection of Chairs and certain other academic administrators; procedures for amending bylaws; and other matters of professional concern.

26.6   No reprisal of any kind shall be made by the Board or the UFF against any faculty member based on that faculty member's participation in the system of shared governance. Any damage to a faculty member as a consequence of such reprisals shall be repaired.

Article 27
MAINTENANCE OF BENEFITS

27.1   No Coercion. No faculty member shall be required or coerced to waive the benefits provided by the terms of this Agreement.

27.2   No Loss of Rights or Benefits. No faculty member shall, as a result of the establishment of a level of rights or benefits in this Agreement, suffer a loss or diminution of any such rights or benefits for which otherwise eligible.

Article 28
MISCELLANEOUS PROVISIONS

28.1   No Strike or Lockout. The Board agrees that there will be no lockout during the term of this Agreement. The UFF agrees that there will be no strike by it or by any faculty member during the term of this Agreement.

28.2   Venue. For purposes of venue in any judicial review of an arbitrator's decision, the parties elect to submit themselves to the jurisdiction of the courts in Leon County, Florida. In an action commenced in Leon County, neither the Board nor the UFF will move for a change of venue based upon the defendant's residence in fact if other than Leon County.

28.3   Titles and Headings. The titles of Articles and headings that precede text are inserted solely for convenience of reference and shall not be deemed to limit or affect the meaning, construction, or effect of any provision of this Agreement.

Article 29
SEVERABILITY

29.1   Invalidation of a Provision of the Agreement.
    (a) A provision of this Agreement shall become invalid and have no force or effect, if it:
        (1) Is found to be invalid or unenforceable by final decision of a tribunal of competent jurisdiction, or
        (2) Is rendered invalid by reason of subsequently enacted legislation, or
        (3) Shall have the effect of a loss to the State of Florida of funds, property, or services made available through federal law.

    (b) In such circumstances, however, the remainder of the Agreement shall continue in full force and effect.

29.2   Negotiations on Replacement Provisions. If a provision of this Agreement fails for a reason in Section 29.1(a) above, the Board and the UFF shall enter into immediate negotiations for the purpose of arriving at a mutually satisfactory replacement for such provision.

29.3   Effect of Passage of Law. Any provision of this Agreement that is contrary to law, but becomes legal during the term of this Agreement, shall be reinstated consistent with such legislation.

29.4   Intent. The above provisions are not intended by the Board and the UFF to constitute a contractual or any other recognition or grant of authority by either party that subsequent legislation can invalidate any provision of this Agreement. The Board and the UFF intend for the language of the above provisions to recognize the possibility, regardless of their intentions, that subsequently enacted legislation may attempt, be construed, be interpreted or be applied to invalidate a provision of this Agreement, and the Board and the UFF may choose not to challenge said legislation or its application, or one or both Board and the UFF may challenge said legislation or its application without success.

29.5   Legislative Action. The Board and the UFF agree not to seek the enactment of legislation for the purpose of avoiding an obligation arising from this contract. The Board and the UFF recognize the right of the parties to express opinions with regard to the delivery of higher education in the State of Florida.

Article 30
AMENDMENT AND DURATION

30.1   Effective Date. The Agreement shall become effective on the date it is ratified by both parties and remain in effect through June 30, 2016.

30.2   Amendments. In the event the Board and the UFF negotiate a mutually acceptable amendment to this Agreement, such amendment shall be put in writing and become part of this Agreement upon ratification by both parties.

30.3   Notice. Either party may reopen articles in accordance with Section 30.1 by providing written notice by April 1st of the contract year. Notices hereunder shall be provided in writing and shall be addressed to the President of the FSU Chapter of the United Faculty of Florida and to the Board of Trustees of Florida State University at the Human Resources Office.

30.4   Negotiations for the agreement term July 1, 2016 through June 30, 2019 shall begin no later than March 1, 2016.

(a) Parties shall inform the other party in writing by February 1, 2016 of any articles to be negotiated.

(b) Any article not listed shall be maintained unchanged in the new agreement.

Article 31
TOTALITY OF AGREEMENT

(c) Any article may be opened for negotiation at a later date by mutual agreement of the parties.

Article 31
TOTALITY OF AGREEMENT

31.1   Limitation.

(a) The Board and the UFF acknowledge that during the negotiations that resulted in the Agreement, the Board and the UFF had the unlimited right and opportunity to present demands and proposals with respect to any and all matters lawfully subject to collective bargaining.

(b) The Board and the UFF further acknowledge that all of the understandings and agreements arrived at thereby are set forth in this Agreement, and that it shall constitute the entire and sole Agreement between the parties for its duration.

31.2   Obligation to Bargain Changes. During the term of this Agreement, the Board and the UFF agree that the other shall not be obligated to bargain collectively with respect to any subject or matter covered by this Agreement. Notwithstanding these limitations, if the Board seeks to change a term or condition of employment for faculty, the Board shall be obligated to bargain immediately the impact of such change.

31.3   Modifications. Nothing herein shall, however, preclude the Board and the UFF from mutually agreeing to alter, amend, supplement, delete, enlarge, or modify in writing any of the provisions of this Agreement.

Article 32
DEFINITIONS

As used in this Agreement, the term:

– "academic year" means a period consisting of a fall and spring semester of approximately 39 contiguous weeks.

– "administration" means administrative staff acting on behalf of the President and/or Board of Trustees.

– "Board" or "Board of Trustees" means the legally responsible governing body of the Florida State University, established by Article 9 Section 7 of the Florida Constitution, acting through the President and staff.

– "bargaining unit" means those faculty members, collectively, represented for collective bargaining purposes by the UFF pursuant to the certification of the Florida Public Employees Relations Commission in Case Number EL-2003-038 (October 24, 2003) and reflected in Certification Order Number 1438.

– "Board committee" or "committee of the Board" means any committee or subcommittee of the Board.

– "break in service" means those absences following which the faculty member is treated as a new faculty member for purposes of computing seniority and years of service.

– "college/unit" means a college or a comparable administrative unit generally equivalent in size and character to a college.

– "continuous service" means employment uninterrupted by a break in service. For academic year faculty members (9 month), one year of continuous service is equivalent to the nine (9) month employment period.

– "days" means calendar days.

– "dean" means the principal administrator of a college or of a comparable administrative unit generally equivalent in size and character to a college.

– "department chair" means the principal administrator of a department/unit. In the case of a college/unit that does not contain any department/units, the dean also serves in the role of department chair.

– "department/unit" means a department or a comparable administrative unit generally equivalent in size and character to a department, within a college. In the case of a college or school that does not contain any smaller administrative units, the college is considered to be a department/unit unto itself.

– "employee" means a member of the bargaining unit.

– "equitable" means fair and reasonable under the circumstances.

– "faculty member" means a member of the bargaining unit, and "faculty members" means all members of the bargaining unit.

– "months" means calendar months.

– number: The singular includes the plural.

– "President or representative" means the University President, or a person(s) who has been delegated to speak and act with the authority of the President in the matter at hand.

– "principal place of employment" means the campus location or other University site specified on the faculty member's standard employment contract.

– "semester" means one of the two approximately 19.5 week periods which together constitute the academic year.

Article 32
DEFINITIONS

– "supervisor" means an individual identified by the President or representative as having immediate administrative authority over faculty members.

– "SUS" or "State University System" means the system of institutions and agencies within the jurisdiction of the Board of Governors.

– "UFF" means the United Faculty of Florida.

– "UFF Chapter" means the Florida State University chapter of the UFF. Notification of the UFF Chapter means notification of the President of the UFF Chapter or designated representative.

– "UFF Grievance Chair" means the chair of the Grievance Committee of the UFF Chapter.

– "unit" means a recognized administrative or organizational entity of the University.

– "Unit Head" for the purpose of grievance processing is the dean or comparable-level administrator, as appropriate, over the unit in which the grievant is employed.

– "University" means the Florida State University acting through the Board of Trustees, the President or its staff.

– "year" means a period of twelve (12) consecutive months.

Appendix A
POSITION CLASSIFICATIONS IN THE BARGAINING UNIT

All faculty members in the following position classifications holding regular, visiting, provisional, research, affiliate, or joint appointments are included in the bargaining unit:

9001 – Professor
9002 – Associate Professor
9003 – Assistant Professor
9004 – Instructor*
9005 – Lecturer*
9006 – Graduate Research Professor*
9007 – Distinguished Service Professor*
9009 – Eminent Scholar
9053 – University Librarian
9054 – Associate University Librarian
9055 – Assistant University Librarian
9056 – Instructor University Librarian*
9060 – Teaching Faculty I
9061 – Teaching Faculty II
9062 – Teaching Faculty III
9070 – Instructional Specialist I
9071 – Instructional Specialist II
9072 – Instructional Specialist III
9080 – Research Faculty I
9081 – Research Faculty II
9082 – Research Faculty III
9115 – Coordinator*
9120 – Associate in _____ *
9121 – Assistant in _____ *
9126 – Program Director*
9130 – Specialist, Computer Research
9135 – Specialist, Music
9140 – Childcare Specialist
9150 – Curator
9151 – Associate Curator
9152 – Assistant Curator
9153 – Staff Physicist*
9160 – Scholar/Scientist/Engineer*
9161 – Associate Scholar/Scientist/Engineer*
9162 – Assistant Scholar/Scientist/Engineer*

Appendix A
POSITION CLASSIFICATIONS IN THE BARGAINING UNIT

    9165 – Senior Research Associate
    9166 – Research Associate*
    9167 – Associate in Research
    9168 – Assistant in Research
    9173 – Counselor/Advisor*
    9178 – Instructional Specialist*

Together with chairpersons (Administrative Code: C1) in the following colleges and schools:

    College of Arts and Sciences
    College of Business
    College of Communication**
    College of Engineering
    College of Social Sciences**
    School of Visual Arts and Dance**

And employees in the above classifications with the following administrative titles:
Associate Chair (C2), Assistant Chair (C3), Coordinator (N1); Program Director (G1), Associate Program Director (G2), Assistant Program Director (G3), Department Head (H1), Associate Department Head (H2), Assistant Department Head (H3), and Counselor/Advisor (B1).

Excluded:
Department Chairs in departments not specifically included above, employees in the included classifications with administrative titles not specifically included above, Deans, Associate Deans, Assistant Deans, and all other administrators above them, Administrative & Professional employees not specifically included, employees of the College of Law and College of Medicine, employees serving as members of the University Board of Trustees, managerial employees, confidential employees, and all other employees.

* Scheduled to be eliminated after implementation of the Specialized Faculty Reclassification Project and once all grandfathered incumbents vacate these positions.

** The College of Communication and Information is considered the successor to the College of Communication, the College of Social Sciences and Public Policy is considered the successor to the College of Social Sciences, and the College of Visual Arts, Theatre and Dance is considered the successor to the School of Visual Arts and Dance.

Appendix B
SAMPLE DUES CHECK-OFF AUTHORIZATION FORM

UFF dues are 1% of bi-weekly salary. Please fill out the form below and return it to: Jack Fiorito, President, UFF-FSU Chapter, RBB 244, Campus 1110.

Membership Form   United Faculty of Florida   FSU Chapter
Please Print Complete Information

_____   _____
Employee ID Number   Last Name, First Name, MI

_____   _____
Home Street Address   Campus Address & Mail Code Dept.

_____   _____
City, State, Zip Code   Office Phone   Home Phone

_____   _____
Personal Email Address   FSU Email Address

Please enroll me immediately as a member of the United Faculty of Florida (FEA, NEA-AFT, AFL-CIO). I hereby authorize my employer to begin bi-weekly payroll deduction of United Faculty of Florida dues (1% of bi-weekly salary). This deduction authorization shall continue until revoked by me at any time upon 30 days written notice to FSU's payroll office and to the United Faculty of Florida.

_____   _____
Signature (for payroll deduction authorization)   Today's Date

Visit the UFF-FSU Chapter Web Site at www.uff-fsu.org • FSU Works Because We Do!

Appendix B
SAMPLE DUES CHECK-OFF AUTHORIZATION FORM

UFF-PAC PAYROLL DEDUCTION AUTHORIZATION FORM

United Faculty of Florida – Political Action Committee
306 Park Avenue
Tallahassee, FL 32301
850-224-8220

Please Print:

University/College_____   Dept.:_____

Name: _____

Address: _____

City:_____State:_____Zip:_____

UFF-PAC Payroll Deduction (For State University Employees)

I authorize the Board of Trustees, through the University, to deduct from my pay, starting with the first full biweekly pay period commencing not earlier than seven full days from the date this authorization is received by the University, contributions to the UFF-Political Action Committee in the amount of $1.00 per pay period, and I direct that the sum so deducted be paid over to the UFF.

The above deduction authorization shall continue until either revoked by me through written notice to my University personnel office or my transfer out of this bargaining unit.

_____   _____
Member's Signature   Date

Appendix C
GRIEVANCE

I. Date (Received by University) _____

GRIEVANT(S)   STEP 1 GRIEVANCE REPRESENTATIVE

NAME(S):_____   NAME:_____

_____

DEPT(S):_____

_____

OFFICE PHONE: _____   OFFICE PHONE:_____

If grievant is represented by the UFF or legal counsel, all University communications should go to the grievant's representative.

Other address to which University mailings pertaining to grievance shall be sent:

_____
_____
_____
_____

II. GRIEVANCE

Article(s) and Section(s) of Agreement allegedly violated:

_____
_____

Statement of grievance (must include date of acts or omissions complained of):

_____
_____
_____
_____
_____

Remedy Sought:

_____
_____
_____ (See page 2 for additional requirements)

III. AUTHORIZATION

I will be represented in this grievance by: (check one - representative must sign on appropriate line):

☐   UFF _____

☐   Legal Counsel _____

☐   Myself _____

I certify that I have sought facilitation of an informal resolution of this dispute, in accordance with Article 20 Section 20.8(a), and have attached a dated copy of my written request for facilitation to this form.

I UNDERSTAND AND AGREE THAT BY FILING THIS GRIEVANCE, I WAIVE WHATEVER RIGHTS I MAY HAVE UNDER CHAPTER 120 OF THE FLORIDA STATUTES WITH REGARD TO THE MATTERS I HAVE RAISED HEREIN AND UNDER ALL OTHER UNIVERSITY PROCEDURES WHICH MAY BE AVAILABLE TO ADDRESS THESE MATTERS.

This grievance was filed with the Unit Head on _____ by (check one)
☐ mail (☐ certified or registered, ☐ restricted delivery, ☐ return receipt requested) ☐ personal delivery ☐ other (specify) _____.

_____
         Signature of Grievant

(Grievant must sign if grievance is to be processed).

The Step 1 decision shall be transmitted to Grievant's Step 1 Representative by personal delivery with written documentation of receipt or by certified mail, return receipt requested. A copy of this decision shall be sent to Grievant, and the local UFF Chapter if grievant elected self-representation or representation by legal counsel.

Appendix D
STEP 2 GRIEVANCE

Request for Review of Step 1 Decision

GRIEVANT   STEP 1 GRIEVANCE REPRESENTATIVE

NAME: _____   NAME:_____

UNIVERSITY: _____   MAILING ADDRESS:_____

COLLEGE:_____

DEPT:_____

OFFICE PHONE: _____   OFFICE PHONE: _____

DATE OF STEP 1 DECISION:_____

Article(s) and Section(s) of Agreement allegedly violated(as specified in Step 1):
_____

I hereby request that the Provost or representative review the attached decision made in connection with the attached grievance because:
_____
_____
_____

Remedy Sought (in initial filing step in at Step 2):
_____
_____
_____

Grievant's representative received the decision on   _____

Grievant filed this request for review with the Provost's Office on _____,
(check one) ☐ mail (☐ certified or registered, ☐ restricted delivery, ☐ return receipt requested)
☐ personal delivery ☐ other (specify)_____.

DATE OF RECEIPT BY OFFICE OF THE VICE PRESIDENT FOR FACULTY DEVELOPMENT AND ADVANCEMENT:

_____   _____
Signature of Grievant   Date

I am represented in this grievance by (check one -representative should sign on appropriate line):
☐   UFF _____
☐   Legal Counsel _____
☐   Myself _____
(See page 2 for additional requirements)

Appendix D
STEP 2 GRIEVANCE

A copy of the following documents must be attached to this Request at the time of its filing with the Provost or representative:

1.   Appendix C, Original grievance form filed with the University, including evidence of prior request for facilitated informal resolution and any other attachments.

2.   Step 1 Decision, if issued by University.

3.   All attachments to Step 1 Decision, as required in Section 20.8, Grievance Procedure.

This request should be sent to the following address:

OFFICE OF THE VICE PRESIDENT FOR FACULTY DEVELOPMENT AND ADVANCEMENT
Florida State University
314 Westcott Building
Tallahassee, Florida 32306

The Step 2 decision shall be transmitted to Grievant's Step 2 Representative (if Grievant is represented by UFF, the decision will be sent to the UFF State Office) by personal delivery with written documentation of receipt or by certified mail, return receipt requested. Copies of this decision shall be sent to Grievant and the President's Representative for Contract Administration, and to the UFF if grievant elected self-representation or representation by legal counsel.

Appendix E
NOTICE OF ARBITRATION

The United Faculty of Florida hereby gives notice of its intent to proceed to arbitration in connection with the decision of the Office of the Vice President for Faculty Development and Advancement dated _____ and received by the UFF State Office on _____ in this grievance of:

NAME:

FSU GRIEVANCE FILE NO:

The following statement of issue(s) before the Arbitrator is proposed:

_____
_____
_____

This notice was filed with the Office of the Vice President for Faculty Development and Advancement on_____ by
(check one) ☐ mail (☐ certified or registered, ☐ restricted delivery, ☐ return receipt requested) ☐ personal delivery ☐ other (specify) _____.

Date of receipt by the Vice President for Faculty Development and Advancement' Office:

_____

_____
Signature of UFF President or Director of Arbitrations

I hereby authorize UFF to proceed to arbitration with my grievance. I also authorize UFF and the Board of Trustees or its representatives to use, during the arbitration proceedings, copies of any materials in my evaluation file pertinent to this grievance and to furnish copies of the same to the arbitrator.

_____
Signature of Grievant

This notice should be sent to:

OFFICE OF THE VICE PRESIDENT FOR FACULTY DEVELOPMENT AND ADVANCEMENT
Florida State University
314 Westcott Building
Tallahassee, Florida 32306

Appendix F
ANNUAL EVALUATION SUMMARY FORM

PERIOD OF REPORT (if other than annual)
FROM: TO:

_____
NAME

_____
RANK AND POSITION

_____
COLLEGE / UNIT

_____
DEPARTMENT / UNIT

Evaluator's Name and Position_____

PERFORMANCE OF DUTIES

Indicate evaluation by placing an "x" in the appropriate column for each category below. In the "Overall Performance" section, rate the faculty member's overall performance in fulfilling his or her responsibilities to the University. Average AOR Percentage is based on the annual assignment of responsibilities (9-month assignment for 9-month faculty). The annual evaluation shall include evaluation of summer activities for 9-month faculty if there is a summer assignment.

CATEGORY	Average AOR Percentage	Substantially Exceeds FSU's High Expectations	Exceeds FSU's High Expectations	Meets FSU's High Expectations	Official Concern	Does Not Meet FSU's High Expectations	Not Observed
TEACHING							
RESEARCH AND OTHER CREATIVE ACTIVITY							
SERVICE							
OTHER							
SPOKEN ENGLISH COMPETENCY*	▓	▓	▓		▓		
OVERALL PERFORMANCE**							

ANNUAL EVALUATION SUMMARY FORM

The evaluator's narrative explanation of overall performance must be attached. The evaluator should receive input from both students and faculty in preparing this report. If for any reason such input is unavailable, the report should indicate why and what alternative methods have been used.

Has this rating been discussed with this faculty member?

☐ Yes
☐ No (attach explanation)

Signature of Evaluator _____   Date:_____

Signature of Faculty Member _____   Date : _____

Number of pages attached to report: _____

Signature of Academic Dean/Director _____   Date:_____

*   If "Does Not Meet FSU's High Expectations" is noted in Spoken English Competency, options for remediation should be communicated in writing as an addendum to this form. A copy of the form with the addendum should be forwarded through the dean to the Vice President for Faculty Development and Advancement.

**   If "Overall Performance" is rated as "Does Not Meet FSU's High Expectations," this report must be forwarded with the appropriate recommendations for improvement (including a Performance Improvement Plan, if applicable) to the Provost and the President through the Vice President for Faculty Advancement.

_____   _____
Signature of the Provost   Date
_____   _____
Signature of the President   Date

August 2015

Appendix G
SALARY INCREASE NOTIFICATION FORM

In accordance with the provisions of the 2010-2013 BOT-UFF Agreement, your salary increase, effective _____, is:

Current Salary: $_____

Promotion from _____to_____: $_____
[Section 23.3(a)]

Market Equity: $_____ [Section 23.5]

Retention Adjustment: $_____ [Section 23.8]

Salary Plan for Professors (SPP): $_____ [Section 23.3(b)]
Other (Specify Reason & Amount):
_____ $_____

_____ $_____

_____ $_____

Total New Salary: $_____

Appendix H
FLORIDA STATE UNIVERSITY BOARD OF TRUSTEES AND UNITED FACULTY OF FLORIDA EXCLUSIVE ASSIGNMENT DISPUTE RESOLUTION PROCEDURE

H.1   Exclusive Method

(a) The Board of Trustees and the United Faculty of Florida agree to the following procedure as the exclusive method of resolving disputes under Section 9.3 of the Agreement that allege that a faculty member's assignment has been imposed arbitrarily or unreasonably.

(b) A faculty member who alleges that the assignment has been imposed arbitrarily or unreasonably may file a grievance under Article 20 of the BOT-UFF Agreement only to enforce the exclusive Assignment Dispute Resolution (ADR) procedure delineated below, not to seek a determination as to whether an assignment has been arbitrarily or unreasonably imposed.

H.2   Time Limits

(a) The dispute shall not be processed unless it is filed within thirty (30) days after the receipt of the assignment by the faculty member. If the faculty member's assignment begins prior to final resolution of the dispute, the faculty member shall perform the assignment until the matter is finally resolved under these procedures.

(b) All time limits contained herein may be extended by mutual agreement of the University and the UFF representative. Upon failure of the faculty member's UFF representative to comply with the time limits herein, the dispute shall be deemed to have been finally determined at the prior step.

(c) All references to "days" herein refer to "calendar days." The "end of the day" shall refer to the end of the business day, i.e., 5:00 p.m.

H.3   Assignment Dispute Resolution Procedures

(a) A faculty member who believes that the assignment has been imposed arbitrarily or unreasonably shall, within thirty (30) days after receipt of the assignment, file Part 1 of the ADR Form with the individual responsible for making the assignment. The filing of the ADR Form shall be accompanied by a brief and concise statement of the faculty member's arguments, and any relevant documentation supporting the faculty member's position. This documentation shall be placed in a file entitled "Faculty Member Assignment Dispute Resolution File," which shall be kept separate from the faculty member's evaluation file. Additional documentation shall not be considered in the ADR process except by agreement of the President's representative unless it is documentation that the faculty member requested from the University prior to the conference held pursuant to (b) below, but did not receive before such conference.

(b) Within four (4) days of receipt of the ADR Form, the individual responsible for making the assignment shall meet with the faculty member and discuss the dispute. Within twenty-four

(24) hours after this conference, such individual shall complete Part 1 of the ADR Form and deliver it to the faculty member.

(c) If the faculty member continues to be aggrieved following the initial conference, the faculty member shall enter into a period of facilitation not to exceed ten (10) days with the Vice President for Faculty Development and Advancement before filing the ADR Form with the dean or other appropriate administrator. All requests for facilitation shall be in writing and filed within four (4) days following receipt of the ADR Form from the assigner.

(d) If the faculty member continues to be aggrieved following the facilitation period, the faculty member shall file the ADR Form, with Part 1 completed, with the dean or other appropriate administrator no later than four (4) days after the initial conference.

(e) The UFF representative shall schedule a meeting with the dean or other appropriate administrator to be held no later than four (4) days after filing the ADR

Form with the dean or other appropriate administrator. At this meeting, the faculty member, the UFF representative, and the dean or appropriate administrator shall discuss the dispute and attempt to resolve it. Within twenty-four (24) hours after the conclusion of this meeting, the dean or appropriate administrator shall complete Part 2 of the ADR Form and deliver it to the UFF representative.

(f) If consultation with the dean or appropriate administrator does not resolve the matter, the UFF representative may file, within four (4) days of that meeting, Part 3 of the ADR Form (with supporting documentation) with the President's representative, indicating an intention to submit the dispute to a neutral umpire.

(g) Within seven (7) days of receipt of the completed ADR Form and other documentation, the President's representative may place a written explanation, brief statement of the University's position, a list of expected witnesses, and other relevant documentation in the faculty member's ADR File. As soon as practicable thereafter, a copy of all documents placed in the faculty member's ADR File shall be presented to the UFF representative, who shall place a list of the faculty member's expected witnesses into the file.

(h) At the time that the completed ADR Form is submitted to the President's representative, the UFF representative shall schedule a meeting with the President's representative for the purpose of selecting a Neutral Umpire from the Neutral Umpire Panel. This meeting shall be scheduled for no later than seven (7) days after filing of the completed ADR Form. Selection of the Neutral Umpire shall be by mutual agreement or by alternatively striking names from the Neutral Umpire Panel list until one name remains. The right of first choice to strike from the list shall be determined by the toss of a coin. The right to strike first shall alternate in any subsequent Neutral Umpire selection.

(i) The President's representative shall contact the selected Umpire no later than three (3) days following the selection. Should the Umpire selected be unable to serve, the President's representative shall contact the UFF representative as soon as practicable and schedule another selection meeting.

(j) Upon the agreement of the Neutral Umpire to participate, the President's representative shall provide the Umpire with the faculty member's ADR File.

(k) The ADR Meeting shall be scheduled as soon as practicable after the Neutral Umpire has received the faculty member's ADR File. The President's representative shall notify the UFF representative of the time and place of the ADR Meeting no later than forty-eight (48) hours prior to it being convened.

(l) No person concerned with or involved in the assignment dispute shall attempt to lobby or otherwise influence the decision of the Umpire outside of the ADR Meeting.

(m) The ADR Meeting shall be conducted as follows:
(1) The faculty member, or a UFF representative, and a representative of the President shall be the sole representatives of the parties. Each representative may present documentary evidence from the faculty member's ADR File, interrogate witnesses, offer arguments, cross-examine witnesses, and have present at the meeting one individual to assist in the presentation of the representative's case.

(2) The Neutral Umpire will conduct and have total authority at the ADR Meeting. The Neutral Umpire may conduct the ADR Meeting in whatever fashion, consistent with this Agreement, will aid in arriving at a just decision.

(3) The Umpire shall submit to all parties on Part 4 of the ADR Form within forty-eight (48) hours after the close of the ADR Meeting a written, binding decision as to whether the assignment was imposed arbitrarily or unreasonably. The decision shall include the reasons for the Umpire's determination.

(4) If the Umpire decides that the faculty member's assignment was imposed arbitrarily or unreasonably, the Umpire may also suggest an appropriate remedy. This suggestion is not binding on the University but shall be used by the President or President's designee in fashioning an appropriate remedy.

H.4 Neutral Umpire Panel
(a) The President's representative and the UFF representative shall meet within two (2) weeks of the ratification of this Agreement to select an odd-numbered Neutral Umpire Panel. The Panel shall consist of no less than five (5) and no more than nine (9) individuals, not employed by the University, who meet the following qualifications:
(1) familiarity with academic assignments;
(2) ability to serve as Neutral Umpire on short notice;
(3) willingness to serve on the Panel for one academic year; and
(4) acceptability to both the University and the UFF.

(b) The President's representative and the UFF representative are encouraged to select educators from other institutions in the area, fully retired faculty and administrators, and professional mediators and arbitrators, to be on the Neutral Umpire Panel. In the event the parties cannot reach agreement on Panel membership, a representative of the Board and a UFF member holding a statewide office or position shall select the Panel.

(c) Panel membership may be reviewed, at the initiation of the University or the UFF, through written notice provided before the end of the preceding fiscal year.

H.5   Expenses. All fees and costs of the Neutral Umpire shall be borne equally by the University and the UFF.

ARTICLE 9.3 EXCLUSIVE ASSIGNMENT DISPUTE RESOLUTION FORM
PART 1: STATEMENT OF DISPUTE

_____   _____
Faculty Member's Name   Department

_____   _____
Faculty Member's Address   Person Making Assignment

_____   _____
Date Assignment Made   Beginning Date of Assignment

I believe the assignment was arbitrarily or unreasonably imposed because:

_____
_____
_____
_____

_____   _____
Faculty Member's Signature   UFF Representative's Signature

_____   _____
Date Filed   Date of Meeting

Check one: ☐ The assignment was not arbitrarily or unreasonably imposed.
           ☐ The disputed assignment has been resolved, as follows

_____
_____
_____

_____

_____   _____
Person Making the Assignment   Date of Decision

THIS FORM MUST BE ACCOMPANIED BY ALL DOCUMENTATION WHICH THE
FACULTY MEMBER WANTS TO HAVE REVIEWED, EXCEPT FOR DOCUMENTATION
THE FACULTY MEMBER HAS REQUESTED BUT NOT RECEIVED (SEE APPENDIX H,
SECTION H.3(a)).

I UNDERSTAND AND AGREE THAT BY FILING THIS GRIEVANCE, I WAIVE
WHATEVER RIGHTS I MAY HAVE UNDER CHAPTER 120 OF THE FLORIDA
STATUTES WITH REGARD TO THE MATTERS I HAVE RAISED HEREIN AND UNDER
ALL OTHER UNIVERSITY PROCEDURES WHICH MAY BE AVAILABLE TO ADDRESS
THESE MATTERS.

Appendix H
FSU Board of Trustees & UFF Exclusive Assignment Dispute Resolution

PART 2: DECISION OF DEAN OR APPROPRIATE ADMINISTRATOR

_____   _____
Date Filed with Dean/Administrator   Date of Conference

Check one: ☐ The assignment was not arbitrarily or unreasonably imposed.
                ☐ The disputed assignment has been resolved, as follows:

_____
_____
_____
_____
_____

_____   _____
Dean or Appropriate Administrator   Date of Decision

PART 3: UFF NOTICE OF INTENT TO REFER ASSIGNMENT DISPUTE TO NEUTRAL UMPIRE

The decision of the dean or other appropriate administrator is not satisfactory and the UFF hereby gives notice of its intent to refer the dispute to a neutral umpire.

_____   _____
Faculty Member's Name   Date of Receipt by President's
                                            Representative

_____   _____
UFF Representative   Receipt Acknowledged by President's
                                            Representative

PART 4: NEUTRAL UMPIRE'S DECISION

Check one: ☐ The assignment was not arbitrarily or unreasonably imposed.

☐ The assignment was arbitrarily or unreasonably imposed.

Reasons for the determination are:

_____
_____
_____
_____
_____
_____
_____
_____
_____
_____
_____
_____
_____
_____
_____

_____

Suggested Remedy
(Optional):_____
_____
_____
_____
_____
_____
_____
_____

_____

_____   _____
Neutral Umpire's Name   Faculty Member's Name

_____   _____
Neutral Umpire's Signature   Date Decision Issued

Appendix I
FLORIDA STATE UNIVERSITY CRITERIA AND PROCEDURES FOR PROMOTION AND TENURE

I.1   Scope. This Appendix is a supplement to the provisions of Article 14 Promotion and Article 15 Tenure, regarding the criteria and procedures for the granting of tenure and for promotion to the faculty ranks of Associate Professor and Professor.

I.2   University Criteria for Promotion and Tenure.

(a) When first employed, each faculty member shall be apprised of what is expected of him or her, generally, in terms of teaching, research and other creative activities and service, and specifically if there are specific requirements and/or other duties involved. If and when these expectations change during the period of service of a faculty member, that faculty member shall be apprised of the change.

(b) Promotion

(1) Promotion to the rank of associate professor shall be based on recognition of demonstrated effectiveness in teaching, service, definite scholarly or creative accomplishments, and recognized standing in the discipline and profession as attested to by three letters from outstanding scholars outside the University.

(2) Promotion to the rank of professor shall be based on recognition of superior teaching, service, scholarly or creative accomplishments of high quality and recognized standing in the discipline and profession as attested to by three letters from outstanding scholars outside the University.

(3) Although the period of time in a given rank is normally five years, demonstrated merit, not years of service, shall be the guiding factor. Promotion shall not be automatic, nor may it be regarded as guaranteed upon completion of a given term of service. Early promotion is possible where there is sufficient justification.

(4) Interpretation of these criteria in the areas of teaching and service is straightforward, but scholarly and creative activities are more difficult to judge. Over the years, the Promotion and Tenure committee has normally looked for evidence related to national (or international) standing. For promotion to Associate Professor, the expectation has been that the candidate clearly is becoming recognized nationally (or internationally) as a scholar or creative artist in a field; for Professor it has been that the candidate now has become so recognized. Of course, the evidence for this is different in different fields, and the FSU Constitution seeks to accommodate the variety of disciplinary practice throughout the range of academic fields among the faculty, by requiring that the University Promotion and Tenure committee shall have at least one representative from each independent college or school.

(c) Tenure. The criteria for awarding tenure shall be the same as those for promotion to the rank to which the candidate is being considered for promotion or the rank held by the candidate if the candidate is not being considered for promotion. Tenure, however, is guaranteed neither by promotion nor by previous attainment of the rank of associate or full professor.

I.3   Procedures

(a) Each department or its equivalent program or area (hereafter in this statement, "department" will be used to convey "department, program, or area") and each school or college shall have a written statement of criteria and procedure for promotion and tenure, approved by the academic dean and compatible with the BOT-UFF Agreement. These documents shall be available to all faculty.

(b) Each department shall have an elected faculty promotion and tenure committee, of whom a majority of the members shall be tenured faculty, charged with the responsibility of reviewing the records of all prospective candidates in that department and recommending action on the nomination of each candidate. Each department is to consider all faculty members below the rank of tenured full professor for promotion or tenure, or both, if applicable, each year. Faculty members do not apply for promotion or tenure. Faculty members are normally considered for tenure during the sixth year of service in a tenure-earning position, including any prior service credit granted at the time of initial employment or any visiting time agreed to count as tenure-earning. A faculty member may be considered for early tenure during the fifth year of tenure-earning service provided she or he has submitted a written request and obtained her or his dean's approval for consideration, which will be placed in the promotion and tenure binder. For each eligible candidate, the department chair prepares a nomination binder for promotion or tenure with the participation of the faculty member unless the candidate withdraws from consideration. There shall be only one binder if a faculty member is being recommended for both promotion and tenure.

Once the departmental committee has reviewed a binder, no material may be added to or deleted from the binder except under the conditions specified in Articles 14 and 15 of the BOT-UFF Agreement. This means that after the binder leaves the first-level committee it is complete and no materials can be added to it under normal circumstances, except that the dean may place a letter of evaluation on the record of achievement as reflected in the binder. The chair shall submit the binders of all candidates, except those withdrawn by a candidate, to the dean with a report of departmental committee recommendations taken via a secret ballot and the chair's recommendations on all submitted binders of all candidates.

(c) Nominations for tenure shall include the results of a secret ballot poll of the tenured faculty in the department of the candidate and the narrative explanations summarizing the meetings of each committee in the process. This poll may be taken at a meeting of the tenured departmental faculty during which there may be a thorough discussion of the candidate's qualifications for tenure as evidenced in his or her binder. This meeting is to be held after the departmental committee has provided its recommendation regarding whether the faculty member should be awarded tenure. In schools and colleges without departments, the secret ballot is taken at such a meeting of the tenured faculty of the school or college after the school or college committee has its recommendation regarding whether the faculty member should be awarded tenure.

(d) Each school or college shall have an elected faculty promotion and tenure committee charged with the responsibility of receiving and reviewing all binders reviewed by departmental committees and of recommending action on the nomination of each candidate. Note that a school or college may use an additional committee between the department committee and the school or college committee if the faculty of said school or college has voted for such usage in its bylaws. The eligibility of the dean of the school or college to function in some relationship to and with its promotion and tenure committee is subject to the governing bylaws of the school or college. In schools and colleges without departments, a majority of the committee shall be tenured faculty, and the committee and the dean shall perform the functions of the departmental committee and the department chair described herein. In schools and colleges with departments, all members of the committee shall be tenured faculty. The dean shall submit the binders of those recommended by the school or college committee to the Vice President for Academic Affairs through the Office of the Vice President for Faculty Development and Advancement with a report of the school or college committee's recommendations, the narrative explanations summarizing the meetings of each committee in the process, and his or her recommendations.

Deans in schools and colleges with and without departments have the responsibility to see that the promotion and tenure binders are prepared in compliance with established requirements and the material in the binders organized according to the detailed instructions from the University Promotion and Tenure Committee indicated in the annual memorandum on the promotion and tenure process from the Vice President for Faculty Development and Advancement. Any binders not meeting established requirements shall be returned by the dean to the chair of the candidate's department; the chairman and the candidate shall have five days to comply with established procedure.

(e) The University shall have an elected promotion and tenure committee of tenured faculty charged with the responsibility of receiving and reviewing all binders reviewed by school or college committees and of recommending action to the Vice President for Academic Affairs. Deans are not eligible for election to the University Promotion and Tenure Committee. The Vice President for Academic Affairs shall submit all binders to the President with a report of the University committee's recommendations and his or her recommendations.

(f) Each level committee shall review the candidates in terms of the written statements of criteria and procedure for promotion and tenure. Any deviation must be clearly noted and fully justified.

(g) Each faculty member shall be informed of his or her prospective candidacy, have an opportunity to assist in preparing the folder and add any relevant information prior to review by the departmental committee, and be informed in writing of the results of the secret ballot vote at each level of review. The binder shall include: professional vita; assigned duties; courses taught; evidence of teaching effectiveness, scholarly activity, and service, as defined in Article 10.3; Second and Fourth Year Reports for Assistant Professors; all Progress Toward Promotion/Tenure letters; the narrative explanations summarizing the meetings of each committee in the process; and letters of recommendation. A detailed description of materials shall be provided in the instructions for preparing binders from the University Promotion and Tenure Committee. These instructions shall be contained in the annual memorandum on the promotion and tenure process from the Vice President for Faculty Development and Advancement. Appropriate materials may be selected or abstracted from the faculty member's one evaluation file for purposes of promotion and tenure, as long as the affected faculty member is informed of the selection for the promotion and tenure file. Any evaluation of a faculty member placed in the promotion and tenure file shall become a part of the faculty member's one evaluation file.

(h) A promotion and tenure committee at any level may withhold a recommendation if in its judgment, there has been noncompliance with established procedure or the binder does not contain required information and materials or does not contain adequate information. If the withholding is by the departmental committee or by the next higher committee, the chair and the prospective candidate shall have five days to comply with established procedure or add requested material and documentation prior to final recommendation of the committee. A statement of committee action and all resultant changes in the binder must be recorded on the Summary Cover Sheet. Upon completion of review and recommendation, the promotion and tenure committee at each level should inform the appropriate official of any inadequacies in procedure and in the composition and documentation of the binders. Promotion and tenure binders shall proceed through the process regardless of committee comments and regardless of whether information is missing from the binder, unless the faculty member decides to withdraw from consideration.

I.4   Time frame for promotion and tenure recommendations.
    Departmental, and school or college, committees' work should be so timed that all recommendations with accompanying binders are submitted to the Vice President for Faculty Development and Advancement for the University Promotion and Tenure Committee by the date specified in the annual memorandum on the promotion and tenure process from the Vice President for Faculty Development and Advancement.

I.5   Annual Memorandum on Promotion and Tenure Process.
    There shall be an annual memorandum on the promotion and tenure process sent by the Vice President for Faculty Development and Advancement to deans and department chairs each Spring Semester. That memorandum contains detailed instructions from the University Promotion and Tenure Committee for preparing promotion and tenure binders, and copies of it should be provided to all prospective candidates as soon as it is available each spring.

Appendix J
CRITERIA AND PROCEDURES FOR PROMOTION
OF SPECIALIZED FACULTY

J.1 Scope. This Appendix is a supplement to the provisions of Article 14 Promotion, regarding the criteria and procedures for promotion within the Specialized Faculty, which are defined in Article 9.10.

J.2 University Criteria for Promotion

(a) When first employed, each faculty member shall be apprised of what is expected of him or her, generally, in terms of teaching, research and other creative activities and service, and specifically if there are specific requirements and/or other duties involved. If and when these expectations change during the period of service of a faculty member, that faculty member shall be apprised of the change.

(b) Promotion. Promotion in the Specialized Faculty ranks is attained through meritorious performance of assigned duties in the faculty member's present position.

(1) Promotion to the second rank in each track shall be based on recognition of demonstrated effectiveness in the areas of assigned duties.

(2) Promotion to the third rank in each track shall be based on superior performance in the areas of assigned duties.

(3) Promotion decisions shall take into account the following:
   a. annual evaluations
   b. annual assignments
   c. fulfillment of the department/unit written promotion criteria in relation to the assignment
   d. evidence of sustained effectiveness relative to opportunity and according to assignment
   e. for the Teaching Faculty track:
      i. evidence of well-planned and delivered courses
      ii. summaries of data from Student Perceptions of Teaching (SPOT) questionnaires
      iii. letters from faculty members who have conducted peer evaluations of the candidate's teaching
      iv. ability to teach multiple courses within a discipline/major
      v. other teaching-related activities, such as instructional innovation, involvement in curriculum development, authorship of educational materials, and participation in professional organizations related to the area of instruction
   f. for the Instructional Support track:
      i. evidence of contributions in support of instruction, as attested to by internal letters from faculty members at FSU

ii. other instructional support activities, as described in J.2(b)(3)e5

    g. for Research Faculty or Curator track:

i. scholarly or creative accomplishments of high quality, appropriate to the field, in the form of books and peer-reviewed scholarly publications

ii. success in obtaining external funding, as principal investigator or co-principal investigator on grants

iii. recognized standing in the discipline and profession, as attested to by letters from outstanding scholars outside the university

iv. other research-related activities, such as those described in 10.3(c)

    h. for Research Support Faculty

i. evidence of contributions in support of research, as attested to by internal letters from collaborators at FSU

ii. other research-related activities, such as those described in 10.3(c) and in J.2(b)(3)g

    i. for University Librarian and Information Specialties track

i. demonstrated excellence in the candidate's specialized area of librarianship

ii. participation in continuing education in the form of appropriate academic course work, workshops, institutes or conferences

iii. participation or membership in professional associations

iv. attainment of an advanced degree

v. publications

vi. evidence of commitment to the service concerns of the University or the community

(5) Although the period of time in a given rank is normally five years, demonstrated merit, not years of service, shall be the guiding factor. Promotion shall not be automatic, nor may it be regarded as guaranteed upon completion of a given term of service. Early promotion is possible where there is sufficient justification.

(6) Specialized faculty members who have been assigned an administrative code shall be subject to the normal promotion criteria and procedures for the applicable rank. They may not substitute performance of their administrative duties for qualifications in teaching or research. The duty assignments of such employees shall accord them an opportunity to meet the criteria for promotion; however, the number of years it takes a faculty member to meet the criteria in teaching or research and scholarly accomplishments may be lengthened by reduced duty assignments in those areas; the number of years over which such accomplishments are spread shall not be held against the faculty member when the promotion case is evaluated.

J.3   Promotion Procedures

(a) All departments/units must have written promotion criteria and procedures for all applicable Specialized Faculty available in the department/unit, posted on a single publicly accessible University Web site, and on file in the Office of the Vice President for Faculty Development and Advancement. All procedures culminate in submission of recommendations via the Office of the Vice President for Faculty Development and Advancement to the President for formal approval. All actions are effective at the same time as tenure track faculty promotions, which is the beginning of the next academic year.

(b) Recommendations for promotion of members of the Specialized Faculty proceed, as for all other members of the faculty, according to the process specified in Article 14. The following additional provisions apply.

(c) Each department/unit is to consider all faculty members who are eligible for promotion each year. For each eligible candidate, the department chair (or equivalent administrator if the department/unit is not a department) shall consult with the candidate to determine whether she or he desires to proceed to the preparation of a promotion binder. If the faculty member so desires, the chair and the faculty member will prepare a promotion binder as described in (l) below.

(d) The promotion committee of the department/unit shall be charged with the responsibility of reviewing the binders of all prospective candidates for promotion in that department annually, and recommending action on the nomination of each candidate.

(e) The department chair shall be charged with the responsibility of independently reviewing the binders of all prospective candidates in that department and recommending action on the nomination of each candidate.

(f) Once the departmental committee has reviewed a binder, no material may be added to or deleted from it except under the conditions specified in Articles 14 and 15 of this Agreement. This means that after the binder leaves the first-level committee, it is complete and no materials can be added to it under normal circumstances, except that the dean may place a letter of evaluation on the record of achievement as reflected in the binder. The chair shall submit the binders of all candidates, except those withdrawn by a candidate, to the dean with a report of departmental committee recommendations taken via a secret ballot and the chair's recommendations on all submitted binders of all candidates.

(g) The applicable director, dean, or vice president considers these recommendations as well as independently reviews each candidate's record and then submits his or her advice regarding whether the candidate meets the appropriate promotion criteria to the President or designee via the Office of the Vice President for Faculty Development and Advancement. The bylaws of a college/unit may also institute a faculty committee to review all Specialized Faculty promotions within the college/unit.

(h) The Office of the Vice President for Faculty Development and Advancement confirms that the candidate meets the eligibility requirements, and then forwards the recommendation to the President or designee for final approval.

(i) The recommendation of the applicable review committees and those of the department/unit chair and dean are only to convey to the President their recommendation as to whether the candidate meets the written criteria for promotion, based on their independent evaluations of the promotion files.

(j) All recommendations (to approve or deny) by the dean, or equivalent administrator, and all applicable review committees, are forwarded to the President or designee for final action via the Office of the Vice President for Faculty Development and Advancement unless the candidate withdraws his or her file from consideration within five working days of being informed of the results of the consideration at a given level.

(k) Each faculty member shall be informed of his or her prospective candidacy, have an opportunity to assist in preparing the binder and add any relevant information prior to review by the departmental committee, and be informed in writing of the results of the recommendations at each level of review.

(l) Promotion Binder.
(1) The promotion binder shall include: professional vita, assigned duties, annual evaluations, chair/supervisor's annual letters of appraisal of progress toward promotion, and letters of recommendation, and may include evidence of the other considerations specified in Section J.2(b)(3).
(2) For all faculty members with teaching assignments, the binder shall include a list of courses taught since appointment to the rank from which being considered for promotion, with the percentage of effort assigned, enrollment, and grade distribution for each course. A summary of the results of the polls of student perceptions of teaching shall also be included for each course.
(3) For faculty members in the Teaching track, the binder must also include two or three letters from faculty members, besides the department/unit chair, who have conducted a peer evaluation of the candidate's teaching.
(4) For faculty members in the Instructional Support track, the binder shall include two or three letters from faculty members, besides the department/unit chair, who have reviewed the faculty member's service in support of instruction, and teaching if applicable.
(5) For faculty members in the Research track, the binder shall include:
a.   Three letters of recommendation from outstanding scholars outside the University that attest to the quality of the candidate's research and/or other creative activities and her/his recognition in the field.
b.   Descriptions of the contracts and grants for which the candidate has served as Principal Investigator (PI) or co-PI since the last promotion or initial appointment, as appropriate, including: the title of the project; the funding agency; the list of PI and co-PIs; any other institutions involved; the FSU share and amount of the funding.
(6) For faculty members in the Research Support track, the binders shall include two or three letters from faculty members, besides the department/unit chair, who have reviewed the faculty member's service in support of research. If the duty assignments over the period since last promotion included a research component, the binder shall also include evidence of the

quality of the research.

   (7) A complete description of materials to be included in the promotion binder shall be provided in an annual memorandum from the Vice President for Faculty Development and Advancement.

   (8) Appropriate materials may be selected or abstracted from the faculty member's one evaluation file for inclusion in the promotion binder, as long as the affected faculty member is informed of the selection. Any evaluation of a faculty member placed in the promotion binder shall become a part of the faculty member's one evaluation file.

J.4   Working Titles.

   (a) Members of the Specialized Faculty may be assigned a specific working title according to Table J.4 Working Titles, by the dean of the college or comparable unit in which they are employed.

Table J.4 Working Titles		
Position Code	**Position Title**	**Working Title**
9060	Teaching Faculty I	Assistant Lecturer, Assistant Teaching Faculty, Instructor, Legal Writing Instructor
9061	Teaching Faculty II	Associate Lecturer, Associate Teaching Faculty, Instructor II, Legal Writing Instructor II
9062	Teaching Faculty III	Senior Lecturer, Senior Teaching Faculty, Instructor III, Legal Writing Instructor III
9070	Instructional Specialist I	Instructional Designer I, Training Specialist I, Legal Writing Assistant
9071	Instructional Specialist II	Instructional Designer II, Training Specialist II, Legal Writing Associate
9072	Instructional Specialist III	Instructional Designer III, Training Specialist III,

		Legal Writing Specialist
9080	Research Faculty I	Assistant Scholar, Assistant Scientist, Assistant Engineer
9081	Research Faculty II	Associate Scholar, Associate Scientist, Associate Engineer
9082	Research Faculty III	Senior Scholar, Senior Scientist, Senior Engineer, Staff Physicist
9168	Assistant in Research	Laboratory Technician
9167	Associate in Research	
9165	Senior Research Associate	

(b) Deans may approve additional working titles, provided they do not contain the word "professor," with consent of the faculty member.

J.5   Honorific Working Titles. In addition, members of the Teaching and Research tracks may be granted an honorific working title containing the word "professor," as specified in Table J.5 Honorific Working Titles, under the following conditions.

Table J.5 Honorific Working Titles		
Position Code	Position Title	Working Title
9060	Teaching Faculty I	Assistant Teaching Professor
9061	Teaching Faculty II	Associate Teaching Professor
9062	Teaching Faculty III	Teaching Professor
9080	Research Faculty I	Assistant Research Professor
9081	Research Faculty II	Associate Research Professor
9082	Research Faculty III	Research Professor

(a) Such a title may only be granted with the recommendation of a majority vote of the tenured faculty of an academic department/unit offering a degree program, in recognition of scholarly accomplishments within the granting department/unit's academic field.

(b) The criteria and procedures for awarding such an honorific working title shall be the same as for promotion or initial appointment to the corresponding tenure-track rank, except:

(1) The department/unit and college/unit that evaluates the nomination and recommends the granting of the title may be different from those in which the faculty member is employed, if the faculty member is employed in a non-academic unit.

(2) The expectations in research, teaching, and service shall be scaled proportionally to the assignment of duties.

(c) Notwithstanding the provisions of J.5(a) and J.5(b), faculty appointed at the Panama City Campus who are assigned to the Teaching Faculty series may use the appropriate Assistant Teaching Professor, Associate Teaching Professor, or Teaching Professor honorific working title under the following conditions:

(1) The faculty member holds a terminal degree in a field relevant to the faculty member's teaching area(s), and

(2) A special Panama City Committee on Honorific Working Titles for Teaching Faculty appointed by the President or designee and consisting of three senior Panama City Campus faculty members recommends in a secret ballot that the faculty member be granted the honorific working title, and

(3) The President or designee approves the recommendation.

(d) The faculty member may use the honorific working title in place of the name of the faculty member's position classification for the following purposes: correspondence, publications, business cards, web pages, and applications for contracts and grants. The University may use this title in bulletins, University directory listings, and other publications. The entire phrase, including the modifiers "teaching" or "research," must be used.

(e) Notwithstanding any of the above, wherever the terms "professor," "associate professor," and "assistant professor" appear without a modifier in this contract and in all University documents, they shall apply only to the tenured and tenure-earning position classifications (9001 Professor, 9002 Associate Professor, 9003 Assistant Professor, and 9009 Eminent Scholar). Examples of published University documents for the purpose of this provision include, but are not limited to: the University Constitution; Faculty Senate Bylaws and other Faculty Senate documents; the Faculty Handbook; college and department bylaws; University rules and policy memoranda; and University reports to external agencies.

IN WITNESS THEREOF, the parties have set their signatures this 13th day of August, 2015.

FLORIDA STATE UNIVERSITY BOARD OF TRUSTEES	UNITED FACULTY OF FLORIDA

John Thrasher, President
Florida State University

Matthew Lata, President
United Faculty of Florida – FSU Chapter

Renisha Gibbs, Co-Chief Negotiator
FSU Board of Trustees

Irene Padavic, Co-Chief Negotiator
United Faculty of Florida – FSU Chapter

Michael Mattimore, Co-Chief Negotiator
FSU Board of Trustees

Scott Hannahs, Co-Chief Negotiator
United Faculty of Florida – FSU Chapter

Tom Wazlavek, Service Unit Director
United Faculty of Florida- NWFL Region

Sally McRorie	Jennifer Proffitt
Kyle Clark	Jack Fiorito
Carolyn Egan	Michael Buchler
Janet Kistner	Robin Goodman
Lynn Hogan	Nancy Kellett
Lisa Scoles	Tom Wazlavek
Rebecca Peterson	
Amber Pursley	

August 2015

www.ingramcontent.com/pod-product-compliance
Lightning Source LLC
Chambersburg PA
CBHW080639180526
45168CB00008B/3234